THE COMPLETE GUIDE TO NEW ZEALAND BEER

KEITH STEWART

CRAIG
POTTON
PUBLISHING

First published in 2002 by Craig Potton Publishing
98 Vickerman Street, PO Box 555, Nelson, New Zealand
www.craigpotton.co.nz

Photography © Individual photographers
Text © Keith Stewart

© 2002 Craig Potton Publishing

Cover design: Jo Williams
Printing by Printlink, Wellington, New Zealand

ISBN 0-908802-90-0

CONTENTS

CHAPTER ONE

WHAT IS BEER?

The magic of beer, like that of all the great beverages, lies in the way it turns sugar into alcohol. During that process the special character of beer is formed, its basic aromas, flavours and texture being shaped in part by the process itself, and in part by the source of that sugar – beer's essential ingredient – grass seed. An unlikely origin for such a celebrated drink, grass seed, but one that may provide a deeply symbiotic reason for the urge for a beer that comes on you as you are halfway through mowing the lawn. Or it may be just thirst. Whatever the reason, the association of beer with grass seed gives it a history that is as old as farming, establishing it at the root of human settlement and what we have come to call civilisation.

Of course grass seed is not what it was, and when early peoples began gathering it, there was not much evidence of sugar in it. But as humans have selectively husbanded grasses for their own purposes so they have engineered a family of grasses from which bread, beer and other staples are produced. Principal members of this family are wheat, rye, oats, maize, rice, millet, and the brewers' favourite, barley.

While beer is brewed from all the other grains, and in some cultures there is a preference for wheat, maize, rice or millet beer, it is in barley that most brewers find the special characteristics of flavour and texture they want.

Barley is also the grain most likely to produce high quality malt, and it is in malting that the beer making process really begins, for grass seed contains stored energy that will trigger its next generation and then nourish that baby grass plant through its early life until it grows roots and leaves to sustain itself independently. This energy is carbohydrate, produced by the adult barley from sunshine by the process of photosynthesis and retained in its seeds as starch, which, with the help of a few select enzymes can become sugar.

Starch is the stuff from which flour and ultimately Our Daily Bread is made, but it is of no value to the brewer, at least not in this pure form. Nor is it much good to the young barley plant. Hard and virtually insoluble in seed form, it is simply a handy way of keeping the carbohydrate supply safe while the seed lies on the ground through winter, but when spring comes, so sugar becomes the young seedling's need, and the seed begins a process that simultaneously instigates the growth of a new plant and changes the stored starch into sugars that the seedling can use. It is this sugar that is the essential ingredient in brewing. Indeed, it is the defining ingredient, for as fundamental as grapes are to wine, and sugar cane to rum, so malt is the essence of beer.

So the malting process is simply an imitation of spring, where grain, usually barley, but also any of the others listed above, is moistened and heated so that the seeds believe it is time to begin growing. The maltster's trick is to wait until the precise moment when the starch is halfway to becoming sugar, then to kill the seed with a sudden increase in heat. It is also the first opportunity to assert individuality over the finished brew, because the degree of heat applied will also change the flavour of the finished malt – its degree of roast.

Malting is a process for which barley is perfectly designed, for unlike other grains, on germination barley shoots do not sprout from one end while embryonic rootlets appear at the other; instead the shoots grow back through the seed, using the seed's hard outer shell as protection during its most tender stage. As commercial malting requires a steady process of turning and spreading so that the warmth and moisture are well distributed for an even germination, this outer shell offers protection against shoots being damaged during malting and the seed being killed before it has had time to convert its starch to sugar.

Consequently, malted barley looks just like unmalted barley, outwardly unchanged while inside enzymes have been formed that will trigger the final creation of sugar. In old fashioned maltings it has been steeped in water and thickly spread on the warmed malting floor ('couched'), then 'floored' during germination, turned with wooden shovels and forks, and even ploughed, a procedure that ensures its temperature is maintained and spread evenly through the whole mass of grain for a period of about ten days. At this point the 'green' barley is roasted in a kiln, from which it emerges looking pretty much as it did originally, for the only outward sign of change, a growth of tiny roots from one end of each grain, has been knocked off so it shows no obvious signs of the dramatic changes that have gone on within.

What is inside the husk is only part way to what the brewer needs, for the starch has been chemically changed but is not yet sugar, and while the barley has been softened and given its characteristic warm, toasty flavour, it requires further processing before it can contribute to brewing. This ability to partially process grain is a huge advantage to brewers, because they are able to store the annual crop and use it at their leisure throughout the year, unlike winemakers who must harvest and process their entire production at vintage time.

The next stage, turning the starch into sugars ready for fermentation, is the first part of brewing to actually take place in a brewery, for most modern brewers do not malt their own barley, but buy it in from malting companies close to where the grain is grown. Indeed malt's readily transportable and easily stored nature has given brewers almost universal choice in their selection of malt, for it can be shipped anywhere in the world, and is. This does make selection of malt even more influential on the final beer taste than it was when only local maltings provided a source for brewers, and is the first important decision brewers make in shaping the character, and particularly the quality, of their beer.

Character and flavour are influenced by the type of grain used for the malt. Most brewers prefer barley, although wheat and other grains like rye are not uncommon, and even rice is favoured where light, bland beers are made. The nutritional value of the grain is also a factor, as true lagers demand more food from the malt for their rich yeast foundation than do darker, maltier beers. The degree of heat applied to the grain, that is, the level of roasting it receives at the malting stage, also has a profound influence on the final aroma and taste of the beer, with highly roasted, dark beers having more of the chocolate, toast and coffee character than the typically warm, sweetish malt flavour found in classic ales.

At the brewery the first step in making beer is to produce a warm slurry known as mash, by grinding the malt to a coarse texture and mixing it with water. This is the second seminal decision in defining the beer's character, for water is the foundation of all good beer, dictating much of its character. In water is the source of regional beer styles, for the deep well water that is used by brewers to ensure beer's purity is also infused with a cocktail of chemicals extracted as the water passes over and through local subterranean rocks.

Consequently, traditional European brewing reputations are closely linked to the character of regional water. In England, noted for its firm flavoured, bitter beers, the water is 'hard', making for crisp pale beers in Burton-on-Trent, where the water is high in calcium sulphate. In Kent and southeast England where the water has a good measure of calcium chloride along with calcium sulphate, the beers are similar, but softer than their northern cousins. Conversely, the Czech Republic and Slovakia's abiding fame as one of the great brewing cultures is firmly based on their sources of 'soft' water, which permits greater carbon dioxide absorption, delivering a creamier head and a richer textured palate. Whatever its character, water for the mash is a key contributor.

The coarsely ground malt, called grist, also demands a high degree of craft from the brewer. It must not be so fine that it could cause the final brew to be cloudy, yet it must be crushed enough to release those critical, partially transformed starches into the water and eliminate some of the malt's less savoury components. Hot water at around 69°C is then added to the grist malt to make mash, hot enough to stimulate the enzymes in the malt to convert its starches into precious sugar. This sugar is mostly maltose, and there is also some dextrin, a slightly gluey carbohydrate that adds texture to the final brew.

Most of the process in an old-fashioned brewery is by infusion in a vessel called a mash tun, where the mash is steeped in hot water for up to two hours and then drained. Modern brewers are less likely to use this system, favouring the more efficient decoction method, which lasts up to eight hours, during which batches of mash are removed and heated up to 76°C and returned to the mash tun. Once the process is complete, the mash is transferred to a lauter tun where a system of rotating tynes break up the mash ensuring an even distribution of enzyme action throughout the whole load. The sweet liquid or 'wort' is now drawn off the spent grist, and it has one more key ingredient added – hops.

For many people it is hops, not malt, that define beer, because the wonderful aroma of hops and their characteristic bitterness are more obvious to the occasional beer drinker than the subtle turns of flavour that malt can manage. Certainly, it is hops that make beer a great drink, rather than just a thirst quencher, for the cones (flowers, sometimes called catkins) of the hop plant are what give beer its classic fragrance, its bitter tang, and most importantly, its balance, serving as a counter to the sweet, biscuity ripeness of malt.

Hops are also a preservative and, for longer than beer has been made, many medicinal and mystic properties have been attributed to them. In ancient Middle Eastern city-states, they were considered a cure for leprosy, and for even longer have been considered helpful for nervous disorders. They are also considered a sedative that encourages sleep, and pillows stuffed with hop catkins were a very popular cure for insomnia before sleeping pills made their appearance; the hop pillow, when warm, is also said to be a cure for earache.

Besides making people feel at ease with themselves and the world, hops give beer its distinctive aroma and flavour, as well as serving as a preservative and contributing to the mechanics of the brewing process. Hops encourage yeasts to ferment, and many bakers working with indigenous (wild) yeasts rather than cultured forms use hop water to start their bread ferments. The high phenolic level in hops – those tannins that impart some of its characteristic bitterness – also help clarify the wort, encouraging the unwanted, heavier sediments, usually proteins, to settle out before they can interfere with a smooth fermentation.

The hops are added at the stage of the brewing process when wort and hops are boiled together in huge kettles. Some producers will add other sugars to the wort now, although traditionally maltose extracted from malted grain is the only sugar permitted in the brewing process, at least in countries that still abide by purity laws that regulate their brewing, in some cases having done so for as long as 500 years. However, many breweries simply add cane sugar to water to make a basic wort, as it is easier and generally cheaper. More common is the use of a nominal amount of malt to produce a lightly flavoured wort, which is then 'improved' with cane sugar. Whatever the process, using sugar other than that produced by malted grain fundamentally changes the nature of the product. Beer, by definition, is made from malted grain, and any other source of sugar may be more efficient, more profitable or even produce more pleasant flavours – but whatever the reason, any beverage in which non-malt sugar is the predominant source, is no longer beer.

That issue aside, the wort and its charge of hops are now boiled together in a huge kettle, often made of copper, effectively sterilising the liquid, killing any bacteria present, as well as the enzymes that were active

Hop cones are what give beer its classic fragrance, bitter tang and its balance, serving as a counter to the sweet biscuity ripeness of malt.
(Courtesy of New Zealand Hop Marketing Board)

in the malt, immediately preventing them from continuing their sugar changing activities. The heat also extracts all of the essential flavours and phenolics from the hops, giving the beer most of its bitterness and some of its hop flavour. However, the most fragrant aspects of hop aroma, as well as some of its finest flavours, are volatile and are boiled off during this process. Many brewers restore them by adding more hops at the end of the boil, so they steep in the cooling liquid, or by dry hopping. This can take place at the hop back, a sieve that strains sediment from the kettle as it is drained, by filling the hop back with fresh hops. Or hops can be added to the beer as it ages, before it is bottled.

The details of hopping are as varied as breweries and their beers are, for hops are the most obvious influence brewers have on the character, aroma and flavour of the beers they make. Hops are to brewers what grape varieties are to winemakers, albeit with a narrower range of smells, flavours, textural qualities and performance. Their particular characteristics and the way they are handled influence the beer, but so too does the place they are grown. Of all the aspects of modern brewing, with chemically adjusted water and imported malts having a standardising influence on brewing worldwide, hops can still be indicators of regional beer styles.

Practically, hops are used for two purposes: to add bitterness and texture, and for aroma and flavour. For each beer a different variety of hop can be used, or a number of varieties. Bitterness is primarily contributed during the boil, while aroma and flavour are added later.

The principal hop varieties used for classic beer styles around the world are:

BREWER'S GOLD
English variety, used almost exclusively for bitterness.

CASCADE
American hop, used for aroma as well as bitterness. Has an almost minty, pine-like character as well as a bristly feel.

CLUSTER
America's bitterness hop.

FUGGLES
English hop. Dual purpose, with fine bitterness qualities and a soft fragrance, slightly sweet and floral with a hint of liquorice.

GOLDINGS
English. Dual purpose but more often used for aroma and flavour, with its warm, slightly wild character and rich fragrance.

GREEN BULLET
New Zealand hop, very aromatic, zesty variety.

HALLERTAU (MITTELFRÜH)
Germany's classic, delicate, fragrant, floral hop used primarily for aroma and flavour.

HERSBRUCKER
Big, ripe aromas are typical of this dual purpose variety from Germany.

MOUNT HOOD
Slightly spicy, fragrant American variety used for aroma.

NORTHERN BREWER
Muscular British variety used for bitterness.

PRIDE OF RINGWOOD
Hard nosed Australian variety, dual purpose but with reserved aromatics.

Hop picking in the 1940s, on Mr McIngle's property at Motueka, near Nelson. (Courtesy of Archives New Zealand, AAQT 6439/2 A5583–A28661)

RECORD
Dual purpose British variety with a fine aroma, slightly flowery, with strong bitterness.

SAAZ
The great Czech hop from Zatec that gives its pretty floral aromas to the great beers of Pilsen. Has fine bitterness, clean flavour.

SPALT
German aroma variety, herbal and slightly citrus/floral. Very fine.

STICKLEBRACT
New Zealand variety, brisk and herbal/zesty aromas, bright flavour.

Now that the malt and hops have been melded together, the sweet, flavoury wort is ready for the final and crucial stage – fermentation. Quite simply, the sugar will be fermented by yeasts. These yeasts are usually from specifically cultivated batches that brewers develop by collecting samples from spent fermentation to which they may add a little yeast from pure, laboratory cultured strains to maintain vigour. Different yeasts contribute additional aromas and flavours, and the nurturing of individual yeasts is an essential part of the brewing craft, a key ingredient in the changing character of beers from brewery to brewery.

Yeast actually eats sugar in the wort, indeed it gorges on it in an orgy of feasting, excreting alcohol and carbon dioxide gas as it goes. Not a process pretty to dwell on, but it is the basis of all drinks containing alcohol, and its organic nature is both a boon and a curse. For while it has the advantage of introducing all sorts of pleasant aromas, flavours and subtleties as well as producing alcohol, at times it can become a rogue beyond any control, turning beer sour or putrid for no apparent reason other than yeast's capricious mood. Science has provided many insights into the wayward romance of yeast, but no conclusive answers to all its riddles. There are simply too many members of the family with a propensity to breed and evolve in myriad directions that leave chaos in their wake. At best, brewers can only hope to husband yeast in the right direction and trust that its promiscuity adds interest to the beer.

All things being equal, and the yeast happy, when all the sugar has been used up we have an alcoholic beverage and brewing is finished. At this point, it usually undergoes a period of storage, during which it is 'conditioned', gaining texture and balance through a gentle settling process. In some beers, lager for example, this process takes weeks. In others, especially strong beers, months are more appropriate. Some beers, lagers in particular, are conditioned in large tanks, others are cask conditioned, and many are bottle conditioned. Most are at some stage clarified, filtered and packed before they are sent to the consumer.

The alcoholic strength will be dependent on the sugar content of the wort before fermentation began, and in British brewspeak this is referred to as Original Gravity, in most of Europe as Balling or Plato, each named according to the system of measuring. None are especially relevant to beer drinkers, unless they like to show off their brewing knowledge, but the range of beer strength has weak beer at approximately 3.5% alcohol by volume, a strong one in the region of 8%. There will always be beers below and above these.

Sounds simple, but it rarely is. While the selection of water, malt and hops, and the ways in which they are processed are all instrumental in the individual nature of each beer, yeast too makes a major contribution to beer's ultimate character. This is not just in the idiosyncratic tendencies of yeast to react in unpredictable ways, but in the three different types of yeast that are used for brewing different types of beer.

Like the grasses discussed at the beginning of this chapter, yeast has been cultivated by humans to perform specific roles while retaining its essential character and function. Just as rice, wheat and barley are all types of grass seed, so yeasts make bread rise, ferment wine and brew beer. And within the category of brewing yeasts there are three families, each producing different sorts of beer. These are:

- top fermentation yeasts
- bottom fermentation yeasts
- lambic yeasts.

Lambic yeasts are the oldest form used in beer fermentation. Although rare, they are attracting more and more attention as craft brewing gains a following among beer drinkers. Lambic brewers work on the basis that a good brewing environment will attract the right sort of wild yeasts, so they encourage naturally occurring yeasts to settle on the cooling wort and spontaneously trigger fermentation. Once this has been achieved – and in a new brewery it can take some time before a community of yeasts develops to the point where fermentation happens regularly and easily – the brewer's job is to nurture the yeast community so that it maintains its health and character. This type of brewing is more about husbandry than science, and it produces beers that can be as idiosyncratic as they are spectacular. Lambic beer's stronghold is in the Zenne Valley in Belgium.

Of the other two, top fermentation is the oldest form. It has been around for at least 5000 years, having developed from the lambic system. In this case brewers selected the most virile yeasts from within their brewery's yeast communities and developed them to do the job while reducing their colourful, and often wayward, nature. The result is not actually *top* fermentation in a literal sense, for the yeast doesn't really float on the surface of the beer in spite of the appearance of foam on the surface, but is generally well distributed throughout. It is *top* only in the way it differs from *bottom* fermentation, which, because it is conducted at low temperatures, tends to draw the yeast to the *bottom* of the fermenting vessels, particularly as the tradition is for *bottom* fermented beers to be stored for relatively long periods on their yeast sediment, which, as it has finished its work, has sunk to the *bottom*.

It is for this reason that bottom fermented beers are generically referred to as lagers, after the German word for store. A characteristic typical of traditional lagers is a slightly creamy texture and nutty, tangy flavour imparted by the yeast sediment that lies in its belly for a few months. By comparison, top fermented beers are less yeasty, more malty in character and with fruitier, more complex flavours.

Fermentation happens in two stages: the first, or primary, fermentation being the principal conversion of sugar to alcohol; the second, a tired fading of yeast virility as the party dies down. This secondary fermentation is the one that puts bubbles in the beer, as it continues well after the beer is run into barrels, and in some cases, bottles, so the by-product carbon dioxide gas is trapped inside and dissolves, to reappear when the beer is poured. Some brewers even add a dash of sugar to their beers before they are shipped to encourage a natural sparkle.

Primary fermentation of lambic beers is usually over in around ten days, but with lambic yeasts nothing is easily predicted, and it can be much shorter, or much longer.

In top fermented beer, primary fermentation lasts around a week, with secondary fermentation taking a further ten days to two weeks.

As the key to bottom fermentation is low temperature when the yeasts are less active, primary fermentation can take as long as two and a half weeks, although some times are slightly less than this. Bottom fermented beer is then stored on its dead yeasts (called lees) for up to three months. For serious lager the minimum time is four weeks, for the yeast lees contribute the complexity and interest to the pure yeast lagers that wild and only partially domesticated yeasts do to lambic and top fermented beers.

Good beer is a special beverage, a product of craft, and one of the longest cooperative ventures between humans and nature that we know of. It is also one of those special creations that reflects place, that mix of land care and culture that marks individual communities around the globe, even as it is one of the most truly international products of the modern world. When we drink it in recognition of these qualities, giving every glass the chance to show us all its aromas, flavours and subtle twists of character, it is easy to understand why we have been drinking beer for 10,000 years.

Beer bottle, Cowie & Co. Brewery, Dunedin.
(Courtesy of Hocken Library, 80/1441)

CHAPTER TWO

THE DEVELOPMENT OF BEER

Just when the first beer was made, nobody knows. Five thousand years ago, at least; probably 10,000, maybe even more. The only thing we know for sure is that beer is old, and that sipping on a glass of New Zealand beer today is a link with one of the most remarkable and influential histories we have. That little gem of information may not make your beer taste any better, but it can make it more intriguing. If not, perhaps it is time to change to a more interesting beer, one that reflects at least part of the accumulation of craft that 10,000 years represents.

Because we have no idea when the first beer was made, any notion of what it was like is impossible. We can guess, though, and the conceptual leap from grass seed to a nut brown drink suggests that brewing evolved out of some other process that had already brought grass seed part way to becoming beer. That process was probably the grinding of grass seed to make it more edible, followed by a natural, yeast induced transformation of this porridge into bread, something altogether lighter and more digestible. So there you have it, grain and yeast together, probably more by good luck than by design, then a similar accidental progression to some rudimentary form of beer.

An ardent classifier would call those early brews lambic beers, because they used naturally occurring yeasts which the brewers 'farmed' to get the best from them – not too different from what Belgian lambic brewers do today. This crude lambic brewing spread across the ancient world from who knows where to Egypt and the Middle East, and on to Europe, where beer settled down to acclimatise itself, and brewers slowly refined their craft.

Note the idea that beer is the civilizing influence here, that barley, by producing beer, is encouraging humans to nurture it. This is not a loose suggestion from an author who has been test driving the latest lambic

Speight's Brewery, Dunedin.
(De Maus Collection. Courtesy of Hocken Library, c/n E1928/33)

while he writes, but a logical extension to the evolutionary model of biology. Evolution has it that successful organisms are those most efficient at adapting to prevailing conditions so that they not only survive, but spread and multiply. Judged by evolution, grass has done a great job as it has become one of the most widespread and numerous of the world's families of organisms, by the rather simple method of attaching itself to humans. By transforming its seeds from self-propagation devices to specialist foods such as rice, wheat, rye, millet and maize, grass became indispensable to humans, who nurtured and transported it to every corner of the globe where it thrives on an enormous scale.

For those who have trouble with the idea that it is grass that chose humans, and not the other way around, it could take a lager or two to get the point, and for those who can never accept humans are not in control, there is the perfectly relaxing alternative philosophy that beer is a gift from God. If you are inclined to wonder, think on this: for what possible reason would grass evolve into barley, a seed inefficient at producing anything of human value, except as the essential ingredient in beer? Is beer the vehicle barley has selected for its survival?

Whatever the underlying force behind the relationship between people and barley, it has been an extremely fruitful one on both sides and has been advanced further in Europe than anywhere else. It was in Europe that top fermentation was developed, giving more certain results to the thousands of home brewers, mostly women, responsible for the vast majority of beer drunk in ancient times. It was also in Europe that bottom fermentation gave beer its Industrial Revolution, and it is Europe, specifically Britain, that is the source of New Zealand's brewing culture.

Top fermentation was really just intensive farming being applied to yeasts, a long slow process of selection by performance. Brewers simply refined their yeast strains by choosing the most efficient examples from their brews, eliminating those deemed not to be up to the job. This refinement could be termed beer's Age of Reason, a revolution for singular yeasts against *status quo* lambic brewing, whose proponents aimed to keep the whole yeast community happy. For those snobs who think beer is in some way a lesser beverage than its grapey associates, this scientific revolution happened in beer cellars at least a thousand years before a similar upheaval in ideas happened in Europe's universities.

The gradual isolation of specific strains of *brewer's yeast* was a huge advance for domestic brewers, because it simplified their regular task of brewing, which, along with churning butter, preserving fruits and salting meat, was an important aspect of good housekeeping when you lived 1300 years away from a decent supermarket. Not that efficient yeast was an overnight development. It was an accumulation of observations and selections that covered generations and a wide geographic range, but its advantages, even from this distance, must have been huge.

Much of the development work in brewing went on in monasteries, which had become repositories of knowledge and scientific endeavour in the chaotic centuries following the collapse of Roman order in Europe. This was the case for gustatory sciences such as beer, wine and spirits as much as it was for the more cerebral pursuits of philosophy and physics. Indeed, monasteries were probably the first 'industrial' breweries in the sense that they made for a wider community than just the household and often sold beer to help fund their diverse operations. However, the constraints of propriety imposed on monastic hospitality inevitably saw taverns replacing monasteries as public drinking places, and by the end of the first millennium Dunstan's famous edicts to the clergy included, at number 30: *Let no priest drink at taverns as secular men do.*

Not that the clergy had a problem finding a decent pint if they stayed away from taverns, for they not only had the brewing prowess of numerous monasteries to call on, they were also receiving more than their share of beer in rent for the lands they held. Beer was an enormously valuable agricultural product, an important item of trade often used to pay the landlord his rent as well as being traded to merchants for supplies and cash. Most of the beer sold in taverns was made by local farmers when it was not brewed on the premises, farmers who grew and malted the barley before they did the brewing. Beer making then was the essence of family enterprise and craft, with men ploughing the fields, reaping and malting, while women sowed seed, threshed and brewed the beer.

The improved efficiency of yeast was good for everyone, and as lambic yeasts lost favour so there was a trend away from heavily seasoned, sweetened beers to a purer form based simply on malt, yeast and water. In Britain this was marked by the fall from favour of Welsh ale, which seems to have been the generic name for heavily spiced medieval beers. One recipe from the period calls for ginger, pepper, cinnamon, rushes and honey as well as *fine wort*, a rollicking concoction that may have served to disguise the 'off' characters imparted by rogue lambic yeasts as much as it was a popular taste of the period. It is not entirely a coincidence that the rise of brewer's yeast parallels the demise of Welsh ale, nor that the last bastion of exotically spicy beer is in the lambic rump of Europe, Belgium.

Hops were another key factor in the fall of Welsh beer in England, but not without a battle, for initially hops were considered an unwholesome, foreign weed. Hopped beer was well established throughout Europe at least 500 years before it appeared in England in 1400 AD, having proven its value to brewers in Bohemia as early as the 8th century. In parochial England it was treated with disdain, and no hops were actually grown in the kingdom for a generation after the first hop-steeped beers appeared from Flanders.

This was partly due to the concern small farmer/brewers had about the introduction of a new crop many of them could not grow. Not until hop farming had proven to be as successful in Kent and Worcestershire as it was anywhere in Europe did the British taste for hops become as adamant as it was in Bohemia, yet for another ten generations or so, unhopped beverages were called ales by the English, while their hoppy contemporaries were known as beer.

Ultimately the value of hops to brewers became apparent even to the staunchest English drinkers, and even sooner to English brewers. Not only was hopped beer more aromatic and crisply thirst quenching than its spice-laden predecessors, it also lasted longer and was more likely to taste in top condition. Quite simply hops made better beer and better commerce. As brewers worked to refine their craft according to local water, barley and the remarkable hops England was soon growing, British beer rapidly developed from the 15th century onwards into the drink we now know – the bitters, milds, porters and stouts found in pubs from the Highlands to Cornwall.

These beers, with one yet to be discovered addition, form the basis of New Zealand's brewing culture, for the first beer drinkers here were overwhelmingly British, and their taste was for the beers of home. The more easily controlled top fermentation process also made it easier for those beers to be made 12,000 miles away from that home.

The gradual development of top fermentation had delivered far more efficient brewing in the form of selected yeasts that were inclined to concentrate on the job in hand. But the fertile environment of a brewery still left many opportunities for individual yeasts to set off their own private parties, creating the interesting side flavours and tastes that many of us find to be the most entrancing features of this style of beer. But when they are in a bad mood, or the party gets really hot, there is always the chance of a yeast revolt and its resulting revolting beer. It took a special set of natural conditions to introduce an even purer yeast strain, with almost perfect manners.

In southern Germany, near the city of Munich, for 400 years brewers had been storing their beer in cold alpine caves, conditions that had encouraged the development of a new strain of brewing yeast. Initially they used the caves simply to keep their brews fresh through the summer months, but noticed that their beers were cleaner tasting and better behaved. We now know through our better understanding of yeast behaviour that the low temperatures reduced yeast activity and killed off most of the volatile yeasts, so that only the hard-working, earnest characters survived, yeasts whose lifestyles were less inclined to exuberant behaviour.

What had happened in Bavaria was similar to the long selection process that had delivered top fermentation from the chaos of lambic, only this time cold produced yeasts that were even purer, intent only on fermenting beer, clean and simple. Low temperatures eliminated those yeast strains that drew on alternative sources for their nutrients, because nothing else survived in the cold caves except the wort, leaving it as the only thing for yeasts to eat. The cold also drove the yeasts to the bottom of the tanks, where there was even less opportunity. Consequently the wort was reliably, slowly transformed into a clean tasting beer of predictable character.

These beers are called lager, which, as we have seen, is German for store, a reference to their origins in the storage caves of old Bavaria. It also acknowledges an essential feature of true lagers, the long period during which they rest with the dead yeasts still inside them. Pure as they are, this extra time on yeast imparts character to their clean bodies, and for many beer drinkers it is this slightly wild dash in lager aroma, and a sensual hint on the palate, that makes true lagers such a fabulous drink.

This last great stage of craft brewing had its roots in the work of Frantisec Ondrej Poupe in the Bohemian city of Pilsen, already famous throughout Europe for its fine beers and outstanding hops. This was now

Speight's Brewery, Dunedin, c. 1905. (Courtesy of Hocken Library, C/n E2603/1)

the human Age of Reason, and Poupe bought the latest technology into his brewery, in particular the measured investigation of formal chemistry that would be a critical tool for the final, triumphant stage of the lager revolution. His technology was developed further by Benno Scharl in Munich, and finally by Anton Dreher at the Klein Schwechat brewery in Vienna and Spatenbräu Munich's Gabriel Sedlmayr. These men refined lager craft to the point where their beers became famous throughout not just Europe, but the world, and their legacy can be found in the thousands of imitations named Pilsner and Bavarian from Thailand to the Waikato. Indeed the lager style has become so universal that one of these imitating brewers, an American outfit named after the Bohemian city of Budweis, now has a team of lawyers touring the world claiming proprietary rights over the term Budweiser.

For what the lager masters created was not just a magnificent new style of beer, but also a process by which a high degree of certainty could be introduced to brewing. In the burgeoning age of mass production that was already shaping commercial empires out of soap and guns, this was a call to profits unlike any in brewing history. The great French scientist and original steriliser, Louis Pasteur had provided the formal grounding for laboratory beer in his classic publication *Études sur la Bière* and in 1883 the Danish technician Emil Hansen isolated a pure culture of the lager yeast at the Carlsberg brewery in Copenhagen.

It was the beginning of industrial brewing, a concept that would create the global environment for a new sort of beer industry, of corporate brewing and international beer brands that could be made anywhere. Technology had already delivered malt of any style required, and hops had made beer more stable, more sound than ever before. Now lager yeast had changed fermentation from a risky undertaking with no certain outcomes in aroma and flavour to a predictable process. Finally, Pasteur provided the tool of pasteurisation, effectively changing beer from being a specifically local beverage, to a universal one.

CHAPTER THREE

THE STORY OF NEW ZEALAND BEER

Whatever modern New Zealand beer tastes like, the first version brewed in New Zealand was probably more like those funky old lambics of a couple of centuries earlier. The great mariner James Cook ordered it to be made when his ship *Resolution* anchored in Dusky Sound after an arduous voyage through the Antarctic and Southern Ocean in 1773. Cook was in search of fresh food and a tonic for his crew, one of whom had scurvy, and so on the morning of March 27th, he ordered "spruce beer" to be made and served to the crew. While hardly the classic beverage Cook's men would have found back home in England, this concoction of molasses, "Juce of wort", and leaves of rimu (deemed by Cook to be similar to those of "American black Spruce") and manuka is close enough to the real thing to be fairly considered New Zealand's original beer.

No doubt other, more dubious inventions sufficed for beer amongst the adventurers, sealers and whalers who frequented New Zealand's coast over the next 60 years, before the first serious brewing began in the Bay of Islands, at Kororareka in 1835. Samuel Polack was a merchant in this outpost of the global whale oil trade, trading general goods with local Maori as well as the hundreds of whalers and sealers that brought their crews to port for some serious self abuse after months roaming the Pacific. Most of the clientele in this 'Hell Hole of the Pacific' were more interested in the roughly distilled spirits that were a Kororareka speciality than they were in the more gentle persuasion of beer. But there was a growing community of settlers who were less enthusiastic about consigning their livers to the nasty abrasions of frontier fire water, and there were no doubt many genuinely thirsty seamen who fancied draught rather than a blast, so Polack imported a brewer from Tasmania and built himself a small brewery alongside his store. Using Sydney-grown hops with grain from

Waimate North and from New South Wales, he brewed for ten years with some success, before Hone Heke's assault on Kororareka in 1845 destroyed the store, brewery and all.

But Hone Heke hardly caused a pause in the rise of New Zealand brewing as the new country swelled with British immigrants. In 1842 Wellington's first brewery was opened, then Auckland town followed suit in 1843, with the first of a flock of new breweries in the flourishing new capital. William Smithson's Auckland Brewery soon had R. Clarke's Hobson's Brewery and the Epsom brewery of R. Whitson as competition, while Richard Seccombe was building his original brewing operation in New Plymouth. Seccombe soon abandoned Taranaki for Auckland, where his beer was initially made at the White Hart Hotel on Queen Street. Brewing was obviously one of young New Zealand's main chances, but meanwhile, back in Europe, another development was delivering beer's third and final revolution, bottom fermentation and its lager derivatives.

But that was some way off in 1860s New Zealand, where British, top fermented beer styles were colonising the country as fast as immigrants from the British Isles. Beer was as important to being British as wine was to being French, and for settlers in a new country the culture of the table is not only portable and intimate, it is also remarkably resilient. While much has been made in New Zealand's official history of the pioneering work of French missionaries and later, Croatian gum diggers, in laying the foundations of the wine industry, beer has been either ignored, or demeaned as a corrupt, overtly masculine influence. But modern history interpretations aside, beer was as emphatically the beverage of the new colony as it was of the Old Country.

The new country was a fresh start. It was a chance to both make a 'better Britain' shaped by notions of an ideal society, and to take advantage of a frontier full of opportunity, with beer a critical ingredient in both. For those wanting a new beginning, beer had two important roles, the most obvious being its commercial potential. In a country as far from Britain's breweries as it was possible to get, capable of producing all the necessary ingredients for brewing and with a burgeoning population of thirsty workers with a ready taste for beer, there were boundless commercial chances.

As the earliest and fastest growing of the colony's provinces, Auckland had four breweries just a decade after Polack's little outfit sold its first

A classic New Zealand pub - the Denniston Hotel, Buller, 1945
.*(John Pascoe Collection, Alexander Turnbull Library, Wellington, PAColl-0783)*

barrels at Kororareka, and another ten years on, in 1865, there were a
dozen. In 1867, 1.98 million litres of beer were brewed in Auckland
province alone, and in 1870 a Select Committee on Colonial Industries
noted that the rapid rise in brewing and malting industries made it one of
the most important forms of manufacturing in the country. By 1881 when
New Zealand's first Licensing Act introduced national control over the
production and sale of alcohol beverages, Auckland breweries produced
up to 4 million litres of beer.

The breathtaking changes at William Smithson's Auckland Brewery give an idea of the scale of development in the brewing industry at this time. Established in 1843 on Queen Street, by 1847 it was in need of a capital injection to keep pace with demand, so Smithson sold out to the entrepreneur, miller and local luminary, G. Partington. He changed its name to Albert Brewery in an imperial gesture of homage to Queen Victoria's consort and set about making it the largest in the colony. In 1861 when he sold the operation to one of his competitors, R. Whitson and Sons, he had succeeded, but the brewery's expansion continued at increased pace. By 1870, with a daily production of some 30,000 litres the Albert Brewery was still the largest in the country, boasting the latest technology in the form of a 14 horsepower steam engine. One of Auckland's principal businesses, the Albert Brewery was a symbol of entrepreneurial prowess and industrial innovation.

But beer was not just a business opportunity, and for most settlers it represented something more profound than the chance to make a large profit; beer represented a better quality of life for all, a tangible egalitarianism. Beer was not just the British drink, it was a symbol for many immigrants of how lean life had been in Britain, where the average price of a quart of beer in 1845 was a shilling (10c), or roughly 20 percent of a worker's daily income. A pint of beer a day was beyond the means of most, and a luxury for the majority, but in New Zealand, where workers' incomes were five times higher, local beer was only 2d (3c) a quart. In New Zealand (New Britain for many) beer was not just considered to be the British drink, it was an emblem of Britishness everyone could afford. Aligned with the similar accessibility of prime cuts, in New Zealand, meat and beer were real evidence of the egalitarianism that had drawn people across the world. Never mind the vote – fair priced, wholesome beer and meat for all were the sort of equality that really counted, equality you could sink your teeth into!

Beer had a third cultural role to play, as the blokes' drink. It is a role overlooked in politically correct histories that strain to present either the foundations of New Zealand family values or a socialist/feminist agenda where men lacking political philosophy are portrayed as either drunks or drongos. Histories that speak of beer only as a noisome beverage fomenting social upheaval and family violence are the norm in New Zealand and ignore the evidence pointing to beer and pubs as one of the few bonding elements of the crew culture that dominated the first century of New

Zealand life. Until 1900 Pakeha men outnumbered Pakeha women by almost two to one, and the men of the 'crews' – seamen, sealers, whalers, bushmen, prospectors, shearers, gum diggers – were the muscle that powered New Zealand's founding extractive economies. They lived in gangs, on the job, coming into settlements perhaps once a week, when they gathered in pubs, binged and brawled, then went back to their jobs. Those men were the template for the New Zealand bloke – strong, formally silent, spinners of yarns, beer drinkers. They were the blokes at Gallipoli and Crete, at Cardiff Arms and Eden Park. There were a couple on Everest, and a few at Le Mans, some at Cambridge and Pasadena. They are still around, at least in popular mythology as the sort of people we want to be – men who deal fairly and get the job done. Men who don't skite. Men who drink beer.

Sadly, politicians and corporate greed stuffed the early ideas of wholesome beer as some sort of egalitarian talisman and destroyed the integrity of blokes' beer for a century. Under the guise of moral rectitude the temperance movement so accurately described by author Conrad Bollinger as Teetotalitarianism mounted a massive campaign against all forms of alcoholic beverages, foremost of which in New Zealand was beer. Although it was the younger, less virile wine industry that suffered most from the attacks (which continue today although with less political traction) the consequences for beer were a reduction in competition and a drift away from the individuality that was brewing's greatest asset. The world's brewing industry was already taking on an industrial shape that the technological developments in Europe had facilitated with the isolation of lager yeast, but in small New Zealand with its widely spread communities and small business ethos, brewing was set to become an expression of community unlike any other. Temperance destroyed that by forcing industrialisation and social stigma on a perfectly respectable craft.

Because it is so easy to control, lager is ideal for industrialisation, more so with the commercialisation of refrigeration technology midway through the 19th century. In 1878, W.J. Suiter's brewery in Eden Terrace, Auckland was rebuilt after a fire, with the addition of a refrigeration unit, although it was not until 13 February 1900 that the first true lager *Bismark* was made in New Zealand at Moss Davis' Hancock's Brewery adjacent to the appropriately named Captain Cook pub in Auckland. After the opening of the Colonial Sugar Refinery at Chelsea, Auckland in 1884 gave industrial

Beertanker, 1964. The use of tankers up until the 1980s, to deliver beer to pubs, was one reflection of the efficiency of industrial brewing in New Zealand.

(Photograph by G. Riethmaier. Courtesy of Archives New Zealand, AAQT 6401, A75387)

brewers the cheap alternative to malt, *Bismark* lager was the last significant brewing event for more than 50 years. Soon, industrialised lager production dominated the beer community and continued to do so throughout the 20th century, with corporate mergers and takeovers becoming the only events of interest in an otherwise bland brewing community.

The burning question for modern beer drinkers is, why did the temperance lobby destroy craft brewing? In the name of social improvement, Teetotalitarianism had perverted New Zealand's social conditions on the grounds that they were corrupted by drunkenness, yet in spite of the lower price of beer there were no more pubs per capita here than there were in Britain at the same time. And the problem of alcohol abuse was decreasing, even as the temperance argument was becoming more shrill. Instead of addressing the real problem of abuse with rational solutions, the Teetotalitarians effectively froze pubs into frontier mode, so that drinking conditions remained less civilised in New Zealand than anywhere else in the developed world for most of the 20th century: they institutionalised corporate profits and destroyed consumer choice. The only answer to the question of why, is stupidity and perverse fundamentalism.

The history of New Zealand brewing over that time is a procession of conflicts between quality and individuality on one hand, and industrial efficiency on the other. In every case, efficiency won, with the possible exception of the introduction of international bottled lager styles following Nordmeyer's Black Budget of 1957. In that instance, changed licensing made the importation of such cosmopolitan brands as Heineken and Carlsberg impossible, and the brewers, who were also the dominant importers of all wines, spirits and beers, responded with their own interpretations of the international style – Steinlager and DB Export. These proved to be worthy substitutes, but any beer enthusiasts who expected them to be harbingers of more serious brewing attitudes were quickly disappointed.

By 1984 just two brewers, Lion and DB, dominated the local scene, and New Zealand's only claim to international recognition was not in the character of its beer, but in the efficiency of its mass production and distribution. New Zealand's great technological contribution of the period, continuous fermentation, had transformed even industrial brewing into high tech manufacturing, and beer was delivered around the country in huge tankers, served from pressure guns on the end of hoses. Progressively, localised yeasts and water supplies were standardised and cane sugar was substituted for malt, in the process emasculating some great local beers such as Speight's and Tui. Speight's was once the largest selling beer in the country, with such a widespread market it had a significant shareholding in a shipping line so that it could maintain its distribution from Dunedin, with Auckland its largest market. Now Speight's and Tui are no more than labels, advertising caricatures of what their beers once represented, but an accurate representation of an industry no longer interested in its product, just its profits. It said much about prevalent attitudes in brewery circles in the 1980s when Lion's newly appointed American brewer Chuck Hahn made a point of putting small jars of malt on executives' desks so that they could become acquainted with their real business.

He was probably too late to effect real change, but with the dismantling of Teetotalitarianism at around the same time as Stalinism was collapsing in Eastern Europe, New Zealand's deep affinity with beer was returning vitality and invention to brewing. As was a sense of proportion with regard to alcohol abuse. If statistics tell a story, then the record of New Zealand's per capita alcohol consumption following the remission of restrictive liquor legislation tells us what a disaster Teetotalitarianism was. Since the liberalisation of liquor licensing began in the 1960s, per capita consumption of alcohol has dropped, most dramatically in the last decade with the virtual elimination of the Teetotalitarian agenda from our liquor laws. Between 1990 and 2000 per capita alcohol consumption dropped almost 20 percent.

What has risen has been an interest in real beer again, in the very inconsistency and individuality that has made wine such a hit, while the lakes of amber mediocrity are losing support fast. With per capita beer consumption lower in 2002 than it has been for over a century, sales of strong and specialist beers are unusually buoyant and continuing to grow. Also on the rise is the number of independent breweries making individual brews, while in the corporate world of DB and Lion, now New Zealand divisions of serious international brewers in the Netherlands (Heineken) and Japan (Kirin) respectively, there is a renewed interest in a brewing culture, rather than a marketing one.

There are now as many breweries in the country as there were in 1875, a sort of retrospective progress that is giving beer back to its true supporters, who are in turn providing it with the respect and credibility that should ultimately produce for beer an international reputation to match that of New Zealand wine.

Beer drinking in New Zealand has never been so exciting. Not only is there a new generation of exciting, interested brewers reinventing the craft under New Zealand conditions, there is a whole new retail environment intent on satisfying customer demand for innovation and quality. It is an infectious enthusiasm that is not restricted to the new and the small, for in the large companies, too, even those that once made profits out of brown, beer-like beverages, the sap of true beer and brewing craft is rising, delivering the potential of satisfaction, not just to the drinkers, but to the brewers too.

For many of the old publicans and liquor retailers, notions of customer service and creativity are anathema, and consequently many of them have disappeared from the landscape. In passing they have taken with them the extremes of dismal service and squalid conditions that pretended to be the ironically named 'hospitality' industry for three generations. Industry, perhaps. Hospitality – only in a few exceptional cases, usually deep in rural New Zealand, frequently in isolated communities like Northland and the West Coast.

Now, instead of braving the urinal atmosphere of corporate public bars, beer lovers can find good beer in any number of charming venues, from tiny suburban cafés to the new Belgian beer parlours being fabricated across the land by major brewing companies, and even an occasional brewpub where the beer is loved as much as the customers are. The real advantage of this situation is that there is real competition as well as real beer, so if you don't like the place you are in, there is likely to be another close by.

Retail, too, is a much more diverse and interesting place than it was just ten years ago, as independent importers as well as local and international brewers offer all sorts of tasty goodies. You are as likely to find a bottle of Kentish pale ale in your local supermarket as you are in a specialist drinks store, and with supermarket turnover it will probably be as fresh as any Kentish beer you will find on this side of the world.

CHAPTER FOUR

TASTING BEER

You may think that beer is the beverage of the common drinker, an artisan product devoid of the cant and pretension that attends elite drinks like wine and fine cognac. Well, don't kid yourself; beer is as full of self-serving experts, pretenders and charlatans as anything that demands skill in its making and attracts opinions about the quality of its character. Beer bores are just as painful as wine bores or philatelic bores, and their lives are just as tediously lonely, and their opinions are about as relevant to how you should conduct your private life as your local MP's are.

So ignore them, but also take a little time to do the beer tasting job for yourself so that you can learn to trust your own opinion. Beer can be fabulous; it can also be misleading, fabricated, superficial and downright nasty. While books like this, beer columns and other assorted opinions from critics can help to sort the garbage from the glorious, ultimately the only person able to let you know which beer to drink and which beer to reject is you.

Beer tasting, like any other sort of tasting, is an essential life skill that we should all learn and practise in order to get the most from the things we eat and drink. Almost every individual has the capacity to taste, with some rare cases of a complete lack of taste buds or sense of smell the only exceptions; so don't be beguiled by experts claiming powers of surrogate judgement on your behalf. In 35 years of running tasting events and teaching, I have discovered only two people who were physically unable to taste, so believe me, you've got the tackle: eyes, a nose, an olfactory nerve to deliver the information to your brain, a brain to receive information, a tongue, a mouth. Hands with which to pick up the glass are handy, but not essential.

Beer tasting, like all sorts of tasting, is very simple, just four basic steps, plus the essential exercise of engaging your brain while you do the tasting. There are no tricks, no secret signs or ways to hold your mouth while you swallow, and absolutely no special training required so that you can identify the paddock in which the hops grew.

FIRST STAGE: LOOK AT IT

The look of most drinks is part of their charm, and none surpasses beer with its flashing colour and creamy head. If nothing else, beer should be pleasant to look at, with a head that is integral to its appeal and character. Also, cloudy beer could be a hint that it is out of condition, but not always, as some beer is intentionally cloudy.

SECOND STAGE: SMELL IT

Smell is a very important feature of beer, of any taste, and the moment when most of its character will be revealed, because we taste more with our noses than we do with our mouths. If you doubt this, try tasting while holding your nose or when you have a cold. Even if you can't be bothered to take a big sniff of whatever you are about to put in your mouth (and I cannot understand why anybody would want to avoid the joy of smelling food) then the volatile components will gather in your mouth at first gulp and race off up your nasal back passage to play with your olfactory nerve. This is the taste super-highway to your brain, rushing every grain of information provided by the bite of cheese, swig of lager or sniff of rose straight to the seat of your thought.

Your brain's first job is to decipher the arriving information for danger signs, which is why it is natural to sniff things *before* you put them in your mouth, so it dives off into your memory banks in search of every similar smell experience in case one may be bad. One would hope that the lager evokes nothing but pleasant memories, but whatever the response you get, one of the nice things about being human is our ability to turn such functional facilities into fun.

Being keys to memories, in the process of looking for danger signs smells also conjure previous tasty experiences, and so the smell of what we are about to eat or drink becomes an invitation, a temptation to the feast, offering the joy of anticipation.

So play with what your nose offers, identify the good bits, muse over the uncertain bits, make a mental oh-oh over questionable portions, anticipate what is to come.

Beer's principal aromatic components are malt, hops and yeast, in varying degrees, and the character of any beer is essentially based on the proportion of each, the character of each.

Malt is sweet, biscuit-like and can be light and mellow or pungent and almost toffee-like. Often it has a mealy, grainy character, like barley, sometimes like wheat, and when it is roasted and used in darker beers it takes on coffee and roasted nuts, toast, burned Vogel's, even aniseed.

Hops are the fragrant/aromatic aspect of beer, and also the astringent/bitter character. You may get just a hint of the bristly hop astringency on the nose, but mostly you will get aromatic characters that range from resin and green, hedges and beans aromas, to fresh citrus and rich hay, to flowers, dried and fresh, and ripe, fragrant fruit.

Yeast is a fatter aroma, sometimes buttery/creamy, nutty, often stinky, sometimes sour. It is not often an overt character like hops or malt but is a complexity that gives interest to a beer's bouquet.

And complexity is a good thing, for what makes a drink interesting is the interplay of its different components, the balance and subtleties that keep you intrigued as you drink, or invite you back for another glass.

THIRD STAGE: TASTE IT

Beer in your mouth never gives you quite the array of characters that it does up your nose. Often what you will find in your mouth is simply confirmation of what your nose indicated with one crucial difference – your mouth feels the beer, and the feel of the drink is its ultimate expression. The light, sometimes creamy flick of foam on the head, the cool, thirst quenching draught as it slides down your throat and the feel of its light fizz, the texture and weight of its body and the tang of astringency/bitterness it delivers.

These are tactile and important parts of a beer's 'taste', which you feel with your mouth. Bubbles and foam are obvious sensations, as is creaminess or silkiness of texture, all of which you respond to as you would if you were feeling the drink with your fingers. But you also 'feel' taste experiences: sweetness, weight and astringency. Sweetness is a sensation you measure with the tip of your tongue – not a taste but a slick sensation – this is the malt influence, and added sugar for some beers. Bitterness, or astringency, you feel with your gums and the very back of your tongue – this is the hop influence. Weight is felt overall, part viscosity, part heaviness, part warmth; it is an evaluation of the alcohol content of the beer.

All of these parts you engage as you proceed through the 'taste' from the first impact of the beer in your mouth, its feeling and flavour while it is there, and critically, what it leaves behind. This is the aftertaste, and, if you think about it, this is where you get your most accurate measurement of a beer's value, for the length of time it lingers in your mouth after you have swallowed, the fading twist of bitterness, the residual malty touch, extends your pleasure. Short beer is a rip off; a short finish is also a sign that it didn't have much flavour anyway.

FOURTH STAGE: THINK ABOUT IT

Really you should be thinking about every stage as you go through the tasting process, but it is the conclusion, the summary of the various parts you have put in front of your eyes, nose and mouth, that gives you the whole beer. Its balance between hop astringency and malt sweetness, between body and richness of flavour, between thirst quenching crispness and sweetness, between subtlety and strength, between big aroma and long finish, are all crucial to its harmony and the ease with which it slips down: the invitation it offers for another glass. Personally, I gauge the quality of a beer on all of these things, but the final measure is this one, its drinkability. How much do I want another?

So there it is, the mystery of tasting beer exposed. We can all do it, with the only difference between an expert and an amateur being the amount of tasting experience each has had. The trick, you see, is in those memory banks where every previous pint and litre has been stored, so that when your local offers its latest Pilsner you can compare it with those other Pilsners you have been impressed with. By opening up the Pilsner compartment in your taste archives, through your nose and tongue, you can say, "You must be joking, tastes like your ordinary pale ale with less hops. Give us a break, landlord, get out the back and make a real one, why don't you!"

CHAPTER FIVE

TASTING NOTES

This is a personal view of the taste and quality of New Zealand beer. As with all tastings of this type the critic is an important factor whose opinions should be consistent, not objective. Of course, I try to be as objective as possible, but I am human, conditions change and the mechanism of sensory evaluation is delicate and subject to influence from all directions, physical and emotional. Total objectivity is a laboratory tool and so is only relevant to those who drink beer in a laboratory, or who think beer is a precise chemical formula. They miss the point, and I must say this book is not for them.

For the rest of you, the interplay between the palates of critic and drinker is important, so getting to know my strengths and weaknesses will make the following tasting notes more precise. Not infallible, but more understandable. So if you find yourself agreeing totally with my tasting notes on a certain bitter, we have harmony, and you can be pretty sure you will be satisfied with the rest of the top fermented, hoppy beers reviewed here. The important thing is you must taste it too, because a critic's reviews must be subjected to the same sort of evaluation as the beers they judge.

THE SCORES

The system used here is a simple ten point scale, because most people have a sense of what a score out of ten means without too much explanation. For those who want more detail, try the following;

10 **10** of course, is fantastic, the sort of beer you hardly ever find, but when you do, you remember it forever. Fantastic stuff, with an extra touch of poetry.

9 **10** is also fantastic, beer that does everything you could possibly ask of it – it looks fabulous, smells exciting, has excellent flavour and texture, as well as the sort of complexity to keep you interested for more than a pint or two. And on top of all that it has poise, a sense that is part balance and part uncertainty, as if it were asking a question, so that you keep returning for the answer.

8 10 is excellent beer, with all the technical points covered, has a balance of its component parts as well as expressing individuality and brewing craft.

7 10 is high quality beer, well flavoured, professionally made, showing its craft and character in a minor key.

6 10 is very good beer, a well made brew in which you can taste its component parts and appreciate the contribution of the brewer.

5 10 is good beer. Workmanlike, complete, with good aroma and flavour, a clean finish and fair representation of the style it claims to be.

4 10 is pleasant beer, well made and satisfying, with some positive characteristics.

3 10 is simple beer, a nice drink without much in the way of positive aroma or flavour. Nor does it have any characters that could be off-putting.

2 10 is a minor brew, a thirst quencher without any feature worth writing about, but competent.

1 10 is the sort of beer you are happy to drink when you are thirsty, although you would not cross town to buy a glass. It tastes like beer, in a mild, innocuous fashion, and most importantly, it is not a bad drink.

BREWHOUSE FRINGS

Address 104 Lower Dent Street, Whangarei, Northland

Phone 09 438 4664

Opening hours TBA

Available for tastings Yes

Tours Yes, by arrangement

Established in Whangarei in 1994, the company changed hands in 2001 and has been slowly changing some of the beer styles since. Essentially a mainstream supplier to bars, pubs and clubs throughout Northland.

NZ DRAUGHT

Light amber colour with a similarly light head. Malty, soft, easy going beer, lightly aromatic, slightly sweet, clean, simple.

 2 | 10

NORTHLAND PREMIUM LAGER

Golden colour with a good head and a fragrant/aromatic bouquet touched by hops that have both citrus and floral notes, with an underlying, clear malt flavour. Good, crisp impact, tight and well flavoured with crisp malt character and a nice dash of hop bitterness that comes again at the end. Nicely constructed, fresh, pure beer.

 5 | 10

OLD ALE

Deep amber coloured beer with a lovely head and an unusual, slightly smoky, spicy malt and gentle hop character. The palate is flavourful, again slightly smoky, almost grainy and touched with bitterness in the middle, growing more astringent to the finish. Has a funky note on the palate, lager-like, with a mineral crispness at the finish.

 5 | 10

DARK ALE

Deep, blackish amber with just a whiff of chocolate in its toasty, nutty, malt sweet bouquet. Malt is again the obvious part of the palate, with a funky edge to it and a rolled oats character that lingers on at the finish. Not quite dry, light yet rich, it is an unusual beer. Something of an acquired taste.

 4 10

CLASSIC BITTER

Light, copper amber with a good, open head. Aromatic hop nose has leafy and citrus characters with a fresh, pure malt background. Impact is of citrus-like hops and clean malt, with the malt filling the mid palate and hops returning again at the finish. Tasty but light, with nice hop touches to keep it interesting.

5 10

HOKIANGA
BREWERY

Address SH12, Waimamaku, Kaikohe, Northland

Phone 09 405 8681

Opening hours Winter: 11am – 4pm, Tuesday – Saturday; Summer: 10am – 6pm, Monday – Saturday (later and on Sunday by arrangement)

Tours Yes, by arrangement

Making beer out in the sticks is an enthusiast's passion, and this wee establishment on the shores of the Hokianga is certainly a passion. Established in 1994 it is one of the smallest in the country, brewing just one beer, and only available locally. A good excuse to head for the Hokianga, but then, anything is a good excuse to head north.

COACHMAN'S ALE

Dark amber colour with a neat, white head and aromatic, slightly herby hop hit on the nose, with a mellow, biscuit-like sweetness of malt in support and a mineral tang adding a certain panache. Palate is nicely plump with malt and a mineral, slightly funky richness, charged by leafy hops that give a long, astringent, generous finish. Big, tasty, extravagant beer, crisp and yet romantic.

 7 10

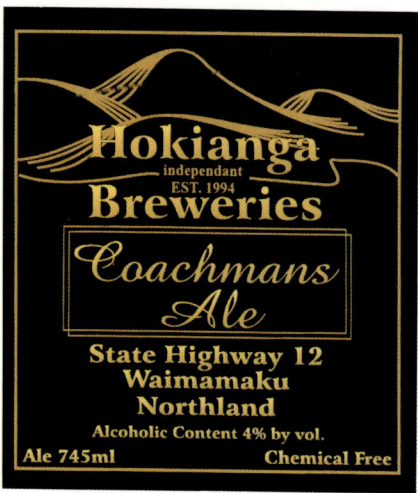

DB
BREWERIES

One of the giants of the New Zealand brewing industry, an innovative assertive company from when it was established at Baird's Farm, Otahuhu in 1929. First brewer was the legendary Morton Coutts, inventor of the continuous fermentation process, but it was Henry Kelliher, who bought into the company when it was struggling financially and set the tone and direction of DB and its Waitemata Brewery.

DB is now part of the Heineken empire, and Heineken is brewed at Waitemata for the New Zealand market. All of the DB labels are made by continuous fermentation, and ingredients are sourced from a wide range of suppliers, local and overseas. Both batch and continuous fermentation methods are used.

Address No 1 Bairds Rd, Otahuhu, Auckland

Phone 09 276 3875

Website www.db.co.nz

Available for tastings No

Opening hours 8.30am – 5.30pm, Monday – Friday

Tours Yes, by arrangement

Address Sheffield St, Washdyke, Timaru

Phone 03 688 2059

Website www.db.co.nz

Available for tastings Yes

Opening hours 8.30am – 4.30pm, Monday – Friday

Tours 10.30am Monday – Friday

AMSTEL

Golden brass with a good, dense head. Malty clean, pure aroma with a ripe hoppiness and pleasant, mid weight palate, mildly creamy, hoppy/malty, fresh. Finish is clean, with a tinge of hops and slight nuttiness. Not especially complex beer, but clean and well constructed.

 6 10

DB BITTER

Light copper colour with a soft, pale head. Delicate creamy/malty nose, simple. Light, soft taste is predominantly malty with a hint of nuts and a suggestion of dryness in an otherwise sweet palate. Pleasant.

 4 10

VITA STOUT

Deep, dark colour with an open, milk coffee coloured head. Lovely roasted character on the front, toasty and nutty. Deep, flavourful, neatly balanced beer with the substance its colour and aroma suggest. Well spread and delightfully finished, smart beer.

 6 10

DB DRAUGHT

Copper coloured, mellow beer, its soft, mild character derived mostly from malt. Clean, easy and light.

 3 10

DOUBLE BROWN

Very mild, copper coloured, lightly sweet beer with a vague coffee note. Malty throughout, bland.

2 10

EXPORT DRY

Light golden colour, with a moderate head of pale cream, lightly aromatic, almost fragrant nose with a touch of hops. Texture is firm, palate has pleasant, mild flavours that are crisply finished. Nice beer, light, dry, pleasant

 5 10

EXPORT GOLD

Golden beer with a pretty, malty nose and a light flavour that hints at fruit amidst its clean malt character. Well measured and constructed, if a little sweet and soft for such a delicate style.

 4 10

FLAME

Mellow, malty and charming thirst quencher, fresh and light with a dry finish.

 3 10

HEINEKEN

Light golden brass with a white, light head, it has a mealy, malt tipped aroma with a zing of hops. Round, ripe yet fresh palate is appealing, with clean malt tone and a lingering dab of hops that are slightly floral in character. Nice beer, clean and fresh, precisely crafted.

 7 10

MURPHY'S

Dark, creamy headed beer with roasted nuts/toasty characters and a hint of astringency on the nose and a dense, creamy palate that is pleasantly suave yet strangely light in flavour. Finish is clean and toasty, but lighter than expected.

 5 10

NATURAL

Fresh malt and yeast nose on this copper/amber beer. Mellow and pleasant, malty to the end. Very light, mild.

 2 10

BULLS EYE

Very light, soft, innocuous, vaguely malty.

 1 10

LION
BREWERIES

Address 111 Carlton Gore Rd, Level 3, Newmarket, Auckland

Phone 09 357 0111

Website www.lion.co.nz

Available for tastings Yes, by arrangement

Opening hours 8.00am – 5.30pm, Monday – Friday

Tours 9.30am, 12.15pm, 3pm – 7 days, bookings essential

Address 36 St Asaph St, Christchurch

Phone 03 379 4940

Website www.lion.co.nz

Available for tastings No

Opening hours 8am – 5.30pm, Monday – Friday

Tours 10am and 12.30pm, Monday – Thursday; 1pm, Saturday

Lion evolved from the efforts of Richard Seccombe, who began brewing at the White Hart Hotel, Queen Street after moving north from Taranaki in 1857. He soon moved to Khyber Pass, Newmarket, where the abundant supply of spring water had already created something of a brewery enclave in the district. By 1861 Seccombe's Great Northern Brewery, with its own malthouse attached, was one of Auckland's most significant breweries.

Across the road at the Captain Cook Hotel, brewing began a year later, in 1862, and Brown and Campbell's Domain Brewery joined the local brewing community. By 1890 all were thriving, but so too was pressure from the prohibitionists and a less than robust economy. In 1897 a series of amalgamations began which transformed a number of successful local breweries into a national beer corporation.

The first was the merger of Ehrenfried Brothers of Thames with Brown and Campell, creating Campbell and Ehrenfried, who were not only substantial brewers but also owned many hotels in the Coromandel, Auckland and Northland. This was followed in 1916 by a more muscular merger between Campbell and Ehrenfried and the Great Northern Brewery, forming the Lion Brewery Company Ltd, and in 1923 by a national merger of breweries into New Zealand Breweries in response to falling sales and advancing prohibition.

Since then, Lion has been one of New Zealand's biggest beer brands, and almost 60 years after the NZB merger, a series of corporate manoeuvres saw New Zealand Breweries become Lion, then Lion Nathan, which was effectively taken over by Japanese brewer Kirin and moved to Sydney, Australia.

LION PILS

Light head, light amber/gold. Very malty, sweet substance to the bouquet. Slightly florid yeast character. Malty, soft, yeast touched, light palate but showing good flavour depth and shape. Soft, delicate, pretty beer, hardly what you could honestly call Pils, but a good drink.

 3 10

STEINLAGER PREMIUM LIGHT

Golden with a light head. Aromatic, floral/ripe hop and fresh malt bouquet, with a distinct toast character. Fresh. Strong carbonation, slightly metallic, resinous detail, with strong, clean malt. A touch light and empty.

 3 10

STEINLAGER

Light, golden colour with a good, soft head. Big, almost minty hop character, herbal, forceful, emphatically aromatic. Sweet, with a touch of rice-wafer, honeyed. Big, positive palate, strong hop middle, floral/herbal with a long herbal character on the finish. Shorter than it should be. Complex, relatively pure.

 7 10

STELLA ARTOIS

Deep golden colour. Big, aromatic, floral/spice, complex bouquet with some classy depth. Slightly spicy, very mild malt and complex mineral flavours; long finish has a freshness and gentle bitterness that is impressive. Clean, pure, long, almost graceful, with a touch of inviting smut at the very end.

 8 10

LION RED

Light golden/amber. Bright. Malty, fresh, English toffee character on the nose with a dash of yeast. Positive, clean, malty, well flavoured impact, moderate, malty mid palate and light, vaguely hop touched end. Pleasant beer, clean and simple.

 3 | 10

LION BROWN

Ripe amber/brown with a soft, malty nose and easy, sweet, lightly malty palate. Short and mild, with a sweet aftertaste.

 1 | 10

RHEINECK

Soft yellow gold with a very light head and faint aroma that hints at malt. Sweet, very light, short palate and mild flavour. Soft, simple.

 1 | 10

WAIKATO DRAUGHT

Originally an independent brewery based in Hamilton since 1897, Waikato became part of the New Zealand Breweries network and is now a Lion brand. It has retained much of its original character and a strong regional following.

Light, copper amber. Smells like fresh chopped ti tree, estery, fruity and floral bouquet. Well flavoured, savoury, light but with character, hints of marmite, with a dry finish. Some nice hops give a light twist at the end.

 4 | 10

INDEPENDENT
BREWERIES

Established in 1990 to provide what were then mainstream beer styles to the alternative retail market that opened up following changes to the liquor licensing laws. Maintains a steady presence with packaged (bottled and canned) beers in retail throughout the country

Address 35 Hunua Road, Papakura, Auckland

Phone 09 298 3000

Website www.independentliquor.co.nz

Available for tastings No

Opening hours 7.30am – 6pm, Monday – Friday

Tours Yes, by arrangement

NEW ZEALAND LAGER

Light gold, light loose head, strong bubbles. Simple malt aroma, light, mild. Simple, fizzy light palate, light malt and slightly florid yeast. Short.

2 10

HAÄGEN LAGER

Open, foamy head on light, golden beer. Light, fresh ersatz nose with a hint of hops and light malt. Very light, malt touched, off dry palate. Soft and fluffy.

2 10

REGAL LAGER

Light gold, foamy, very light, slightly malty, bland beer. Short and very light.

2 10

RANFURLY

Amber brown, light head and sweet, malt-tinged nose. Florid yeast character dominates an otherwise mild, bland, sweet beer.

2 10

GALBRAITH
BREWING CO.

Brewpub in the old Mount Eden library that is an outpost of English brewing sensibility, of top fermented, individual, hoppy beers that are unequivocal in character and quality. Owner Keith Galbraith did his time in the wine and brewing industries before setting up this operation, and the eclectic range of bottled beers and other alcoholic delights makes this one of the country's finest watering holes. The food's pretty good, too, but the beer is the star. In beer terms, Galbraith's has few peers in New Zealand.

Address 2 Mount Eden Rd, Mount Eden, Auckland

Phone 09 379 3557

Available for tastings Yes

Opening hours noon – 11pm, Monday – Wednesday; noon – 12am, Thursday & Friday, 10am – midnight, Saturday; 10am – 10pm, Sunday

Tours Yes, by arrangement

BOB HUDSON'S BITTER

Copper coloured with a brisk bouquet of malt and floral hops with a flick of toffee and a fresh character. Strong, upfront beer with good weight and a solid malt grounding that carries a hearty proportion of hops with ease. Toffee and malt flavours give way to a dry, slightly yeasty finish that lingers nicely. Big, warm, genial beer, rather jaunty.

 8 **10**

BITTER & TWISTED

Deep, dark copper with a creamy, open head, its ripe bouquet lashed by hops but with a thick enough broth of rich, toasty/mealy malt and warm yeast to ground their fragrance. The malt jumps out in the first mouthful, sweet and slightly toasty, but riddled with hop flavours that build to a slow, bluesy astringency that fills the end, leaving it dry, long and alive with flecks of malt flavour, touches of toast, yeast and sweet meal. Big beer, generous, expansive and flamboyantly hoppy. It tastes as if you could drink it all day.

 9 **10**

BOB HUDSON'S BITTER (DRY HOPPED SPECIAL BREW)

Malty, fine, rounded bouquet with a fresh touch and wonderful floral fragrance. The palate is malt based, yeast enriched, lightly sweet and nutty with mouthfilling ease that quickly gives way to an enthusiastic dryness that verges on resinous astringency, although the finish delivers a finer bitterness. Smart beer, with finesse and flair.

 8 10

BELLRINGERS' BITTER

Dark copper colour with a firm, substantial head. Fine bouquet is creamy and aromatic with a background of slightly nutty, mealy, ripe malt and a fresh zip of slightly floral, mellow hops. It smells classy and complete and has a flavour to match, well weighted and smooth from first impact with malt and yeast giving it warmth and ripeness flecked by hops that start as a slight buzz but build through to a long, vibrant finish that is dry and bright with flavour. This is big beer in every way, but it has such style and balance it is never tiresome. Great.

 9 10

BOHEMIAN PILS

Ripe, golden copper coloured beer with a fresh, open head. The bouquet is big and fruity, citrus tinged, almost winey with floral and mealy notes, and the first mouthful is filled with the same abundance of flavour and aroma. The palate also has a lovely creamy quality, slightly mealy amongst the malt. Excellent weight is supported by long, dry, lingering hop astringency. Big, positive, flavourful lager, charged with hops. Fresh and crisp.

 9 10

EPIPHANY BARLEY WINE

Deep amber. Fruity, winey, rich bouquet and a sweet, lively palate that is very malty, warm and weighty with a svelte texture and funky tone. Big, jazzy beer buzzing with flavour and wicked intent.

6 10

GRAFTON PORTER

Black beer, with a light, very open head and a distinctly toasty nose that is alive with floral aromas and sweet, warm malt. Weighty hit of malt in the mouth, followed by a broad, ripe palate with complex asides of nuts, coffee and a dark pungent note that suggests caramelised fruit. All through there is the genial support of sweet, biscuity malt, and at the end a tweak of hops to draw out a long coffee and malt flavoured finish. Delicious.

7 10

IPA CASK MATURED

Deep copper coloured, fine, fragrant beer with pure aromas of crisp malt and fragrant, floral hops. Malty impact is crisp and true with a lively yeastiness and bristle of hops that grows at the end to a long fine astringency delivering a finish of clean floral, hoppy flavours licked with malt. Big, fine, hoppy beer with a silvery texture.

8 10

PILOT BAY
BREWING CO.

Initially established in Tauranga, Pilot Bay moved in with Glennies restaurant and fruit winery at Riverhead, north-west of Auckland, a couple of years ago. Of the independent microbreweries it is one of the few with a good distribution of bottle beers around the country, with 120 outlets carrying its brightly labelled products. Honey beer is an unusual feature here, and one worth trying.

Address Riverhead Estate Winery, 1171 Riverhead Coatesville Highway, Highway 28, Riverhead/Kumeu

Phone 09 412 8595

Available for tastings Yes

Opening hours 10am 'til late, 7 days

Tours Groups only, by special arrangement

PILOT BAY LAGER

Light gold with a light head and fresh, aromatic kick of citrus fired hops. Big and positive, clean, crisp and lively. Dry, mellow hit of flavour that has some charming malt, finished with a faint dash of bristly hop. Foamy character detracts from the delicacy and crispness, especially at the finish, but the hops linger nicely amidst the sweet malt. Bright, positive beer, very light, very pretty.

 6 10

PILOT BAY AMBER

Pretty, copper amber with an open head. Strongly malty, honeyed bouquet with a dash of vibrant, slightly citric hops, and a meaty yeast character which is fascinating. Lightly nutty palate has some middle hop presence but a very light, trailing finish. A great start, not such a classy finish.

 4 10

PILOT BAY SCOTTISH WEE HEAVY

Rich, deep amber with a light buff head. Enchanting toasty, malty nose enhanced by a hint of coffee and hops. Nicely suave palate, with lively, foamy bubble that is not too distracting, and some delicious flavours. Perfect balance of weight and flavour, with an easy, slightly sweet finish that ends with a faint bitterness. Very nice, comfortable beer with plenty of flavour and laid back attitude. This could be a wee Kiwi speciality if we give it a chance. **7 10**

PILOT BAY DARK

Deep amber red, dark, toasty, roasted bouquet, fresh and lightly concentrated. Char-edged palate, slightly sweet, nutty, pleasant mid palate but it dies and fades away to nothing. Very light bodied. **3 10**

PILOT BAY HONEY BEER

Rude gold with a light, fluffy head. Deep honeyed aroma has a dry tang to it and attractive subtleties of malt and a gentle nuttiness. Nice flavoursome palate is remarkably delicate, with a fine honey finish that lingers beautifully. This is deftly made beer, with enough honey to charm the purists and enough beer to please more than a few drinkers. Stylish stuff, light but very persuasive. The perfect cold one, almost worth mowing the lawns for. **7 10**

COCK AND BULL

Three sites in Auckland's eastern suburbs, at Ellerslie, Ti Rakau Drive and Botany Bay, the first opening in 1995, are imitation British pubs, with a range of look-alike British beers to go in them. Has had rather an up and down track record in recent years, from outstanding to decidedly mediocre, but is back on form now that some quality adjustments to its brewing arrangements have been made. Special brews are a feature, and Fuggles is one of the great Kiwi beers when it is on form.

Address 272 Ti Rikau Drive, Pakuranga, Auckland

Phone 09 273 7012

Website www.cockandbull.co.nz

Available for tastings At pub locations

Opening hours Ti Rakau Drive brewery: 11am 'til late, 7 days; Botany Bay: 10am 'til late, 7 days; Ellerslie: 11am 'til late, 7 days

Tours Yes, by arrangement

CLASSIC DRAUGHT

Copper amber colour. Good head, creamy, rich. Aromatic, fruity nose, fresh and clean with momentum. Fruit is pervasive, inviting. Good weight, not big but flavourful, fruity, fresh, with emphatic mid palate hops and a soft malty finish that is invigorated by hop tang. Lightweight but long, with a fruit/citrus shadow. Very fresh character. Light touch.

 8 10

DARK STAR DARK ALE

Very deep, dark, roasted amber on the verge of blackness. Coffee cream head is dense and lightly creamy. Soft, toasty malt bouquet, deep and relatively quiet with hints of roasted nuts. Good weight in support of deep, dark, moderately intense flavours of char and toast with malty edges, hints of coffee and chocolate. Mellow finish with a trailing char character.

 6 10

BLUE GOOSE LAGER

Light golden colour with a strong head. Fragrant, honey-wax and citrus bouquet, clean, light. Clean, fresh impact, again with citrus and honey characters, good middle and fine finish is well-draped with hops. Fresh, pleasant, with a tailing astringency that keeps it interesting.

 6 10

BUXOM BLONDE WHEAT BEER

Light yellow/gold with a fine, compact head. Wheat aroma is light and wholesome, with a fresh edge. Lightly fruity palate, soft, gentle, quite sweet natured beer with an easy, creamy finish. Delicate style.

 7 10

FUGGLES BEST BITTER

Tawny amber with a crisp, positive head. Lovely floral hop and mellow malt bouquet, perfectly balanced with a hint of sweetness and inviting freshness. Very positive impact of depth and malt ripeness, supported by floral, lightly astringent hops. Flavourful, well balanced beer showing impressive craft in its detail and very fine balance. Top class stuff. Long, lingering, slightly lacy with ideal weight.

 9 10

MONKS HABIT ABBEY ALE

Light, polished amber with a light, open head. Fruity, winey bouquet, very clean and fresh. Big palate, filled with fruit and yeast and malt, with a hop touch that builds slowly through the palate. Big beer in every way, with a strong fruit theme from beginning to end and a toothsome, fresh, pure yeast note. Feels decadent, and it probably is.

 8 10

LITTLE RED ROOSTER (SPECIAL)

Red/copper coloured with an open, sustained head. Fresh, positive bouquet, aromatic and fruity, with a touch of floral richness. Bright. Lovely impact, big and ripe, with lashing of fruit and floral hops, super texture and long, soft, malty finish that suddenly delivers a twist of hop astringency that lingers long and brisk. Lovely stuff.

THE LOADED HOG
BREWERY

Address 12 Aitken Terrace, Kingsland, Auckland

Phone 09 379 5395

Available for tastings At pub locations throughout North Island

Tours Yes, by arrangement

Address 39 Dundas St, Christchurch

Phone 03 377 2249

Available for tastings At pub locations in Christchurch, Timaru and Queenstown

Tours Yes, by arrangement

An entertaining mix of brewpub and casual restaurant that has been hugely successful and is the blueprint for New Zealand's contemporary pub. That it has managed to deliver classy beers as well is a singular lesson to the so called 'commercial' brewers that quality and popularity are possible and profitable. Some beers are available in bottles through Glengarry stores, and the range is also available at One Red Dog restaurants. Sitting in a Loaded Hog, you can't help but muse on what would have happened if good beer and convivial atmosphere had been allowed to evolve in our pubs a century ago.

HOG GOLD ORIGINAL LAGER

Bright gold with a big, frothy head of good shape and colour. Stinky, hoppy bouquet is expansive, complex with hints of citrus and malty meal, with a nicely malty palate, tinged with hops and a fresh citric tang. Has a good creamy quality and long, delicate finish held together by some lively tannins. Well balanced, satisfying beer.

6 | **10**

HOG ORIGINAL WHEAT

Healthy yellow, bright and fresh. Light, creamy, mildly stinky bouquet is fresh and sweet hearted, with malt complexities and a real mealy factor. Mealy, mild, charming palate has a fresh edge and a light, sweetish finish. Pretty beer, delicate, hop tingled, pleasantly balanced between sweetness and dry twist.

7 | **10**

HOG THIN BLONDE LAGER

Light gold with a lovely, tight, white, thick head. Creamy stinky, complex nose with a fresh citric tang, a hint of flowers and light vanilla meal biscuits. Fresh and pure depth behind the stink is very inviting. Clean, fresh, pure palate with a meaty, creamy dash at its heart and a lovely twist of hops that builds through the end leaving a long, dry, forceful finish that lingers and delivers detail as well as texture. Very smart beer.

HOG ORIGINAL DRAFT

Deep copper with a soft creamy white head. Mellow, sweetly malty, slightly florid yeast nose. Soft, malty, pleasant mid palate. Easy going, light finished.

HOG ORIGINAL DARK

Deep, dark beer with a light cream head. Very toasty nose, but light and seemingly dry. Light, toasty, soft palate, without much depth or momentum. Clean, laid back beer without much character.

BEAN ROCK
BREWING CO.

Address 79 Ardmore Rd, Herne Bay, Auckland

Phone 09 376 3222

Website www.beanrock.co.nz

Opening hours Not open to public

Small Auckland producer concentrating on the packaged beer market. Owned by entrepreneur frock designer Richard Holden, who was first Mr Steinlager, then Mr Fosters as he fronted the popular success of these two international lager styles for their corporate parents.

Bean Rock is a famous landmark lighthouse in the Waitemata Harbour in front of Rangitoto Island. Bean Rock is brewed by Independent Breweries, Papakura.

BEAN ROCK PREMIUM LAGER

Deep gold with a very malt nose tweaked by a vervy hop aroma. Good, malt rich palate is focused and deep, but finishes quickly, mildly dry, with a mellow malt taste and just enough hops tang to be refreshing.

5 **10**

BEAN ROCK PREMIUM DRAUGHT

Golden copper colour with a light head. Ripe, malty, sweet biscuit bouquet, mellow and slightly mealy. Light, malty, sweetly nutty palate, with a delicate meal flavour and very light, soft finish. Fresh, pleasant, mild beer.

4 **10**

SHAKESPEARE
TAVERN & BREWERY

Once one of central Auckland's printers' pubs, in Albert Street behind the *New Zealand Herald* office and presses, the Shakespeare became the first microbrewery/brewpub in the country in 1986, when owner Peter Barraclough used his considerable powers of persuasion on brewery suppliers to manufacture a tailor-made plant for his Victorian pub building.

 This was against the grain in an industry dominated for so long by the pervasive beer duopoly, but Barraclough was nothing if not a stubborn individualist. In Barry Newman he also backed a relatively inexperienced brewer to do the job for him with the beer, and it says much for Barraclough's vision that the Shakespeare has become an icon amongst Auckland's beer drinkers, and that Newman is still there, making some of the best beers in the country.

Address 61 Albert St, Cnr Albert & Wyndham Sts, Auckland City

Phone 09 373 5396

Available for tastings Yes

Opening hours 11.30am 'til close, Monday – Friday; 12pm 'til close, Saturday

Tours No

BARRACLOUGH LAGER

Light golden beer with a pleasant, soft white head. Nose is malty, crisp, with a fragrant whiff of citrus hops. Fine textured, dry palate is a perfectly pitched blend of light, nutty malt and lingering hop bitterness, slightly floral, vaguely citric. Not big beer, but elegant, alluring.

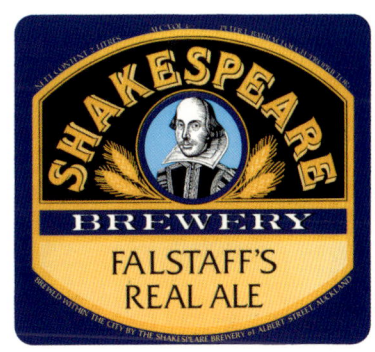

FALSTAFF'S REAL ALE

Copper amber with a bright, creamy head. Ripe, aromatic citrus nose with hints of orange peel and roses, complex and very interesting. A terrific flavour hit that is a hop lover's delight, all richly astringent floral bitterness. Richly malty middle gives balance, and for all those hops there is a surprisingly easy finish, lingering and slightly floral, but not too assertive. Not a big beer, in spite of its aroma and flavour, but perfectly tuned, even graceful.

8 **10**

KING LEAR OLD ALE

Black red beer with a creamy, milk chocolate head and inviting, aromatic bouquet that could be an Auckland speciality, for it hints at Jaffas – orange and chocolate with a sweet edge – with enough depth and crisp fragrance to carry such extravagance. Palate is equally emphatic, rich with flavour details, momentum and muscle, with a lightly rich, creamy texture and details of chocolate, spice, meal, malt, soy sauce and brisk, floral hops. The finish is long, floral and fabulous. Classy beer, by any measure, completely individual, elegant.

8 **10**

MACBETH'S RED ALE

Reddish amber coloured, aromatic, smoky nose with toffee malt notes and a hint of florals. Smoky front palate and good texture and supported by reasonable depth and a crisp, mild finish. Nice beer.

5 **10**

PUCK'S PIXILATION

Slightly cloudy, golden copper/brass with a light head. The nose is fresh and aromatic with spice, floral hops and a fruity touch. Spiciness on the palate too, with cloves and mace and orange peel as well as some floral hops and sweet malt. Long, floral, crisp finish draws the flavours and spice out to the very end. Delightful, powerful, rich beer.

7 **10**

PISTOL'S OLD SOLDIER ALE

Dark, deep, blackish red/amber with an open head.
Surprisingly light, fresh bouquet for this colour, albeit with
a dash of chocolate and toast about it, and a floral, aromatic orange/citrus hoppiness that merges into a Jaffa
character. Excellent palate with good weight, depth and
flavour filled with fresh toast, coffee, orange peel and
malty/toffee nuances, a range of flavours that give a sense
of drinking through layers, the last being a lingering hop
astringency. Dry, poised, tasty beer with class.

7 10

SHAKESPEARE DRAUGHT

Light, golden amber coloured beer with a soft head and a
clean, fresh, mildly malty nose. Simple, well shaped, dry
finishing soft beer, malty in character with a faint trace of
hops.

4 10

SHYLOCK'S LITE ALE

Light copper/amber, very sweet and fruity
on the nose, followed by a clean, light, malty
palate. Light and fizzy, fresh, bland.

2 10

WILLPOWER STOUT

Deep, blackened amber with a dark milk
coffee head and very toasty aroma. Toasty
palate, too, with freshness and good weight, enough
bitterness to give length, and a dry, slightly malty/toasty
finish. Very toast/char oriented from start to finish.

5 10

SUMMER'S DAY BOHEMIAN DRAUGHT

Gold coloured with a delicious bouquet of sweet malt and floral hops that is particularly inviting, complemented by a pretty citrus/apple note. Flavours are not big, but perfectly balanced, fresh, clean and drawn out by lovely floral hop bitterness, crisp malt characters and a long finish that is lined with hops and fruit. Great drinking beer, elegant enough to be impressive even in its relative lightness. Delightful.

ST ARNOU
BREWPUB

Small brewpub and restaurant that has had a bumpy history including a very patchy record for its beer. The wheat beer is clearly a class act, but the other beers suggest there is a way to go before it attracts an enthusiastic following of beer lovers.

Address 43 Ponsonby Rd, Ponsonby, Auckland

Phone 09 376 6373

Available for tastings Yes

Opening hours 12pm 'til late, 7 days

Tours No

ST CLOUD WHEAT BEER

Light blonde, cloudy beer with a stiff, foamy head and slight haze. Fragrant bouquet is lively and spicy, with whiffs of coriander, cloves, cinnamon and orange peel. Palate is light and lively, gently soft, tasty and fresh. A class above the other beers here.

 7 10

PONSONBY PILSNER

Gold coloured light headed with florid, slightly smelly yeast and glum malt characters. Sweet finish is confusing for the name, very short, flat, soft.

 1 10

CHARLEMAGNE PALE ALE

Mid gold, with a light, open head and a muddy bouquet that has florid yeast and caramel characters, with a hint of hops of some sort. Short, simple, slightly sour palate, short and dry at the end.

 1 10

WAIHEKE ISLAND
BREWERY

Address 82 Onetangi Road, Waiheke Island

Phone 09 372 1014

Website www.waihekebrewery.co.nz

Available for tastings Yes

Opening hours 11am – 6pm, 7 days

Tours Yes, by arrangement

In picturesque Waiheke Island fashion, the brewery opened five years ago on the day of the island's famous beach races, and unusually for a small New Zealand brewer, has developed a strong local following for its classy brews. The brewery shares its idyllic slice of Hauraki Gulf island with a vineyard, its café and tasting room with a selection of Waiheke Wines, so if you need a change from the beer there is always Merlot. Not that any of these call for any change of direction at all.

BAROONA WEISS BIER

Hazy pale gold with a nice head and delightfully delicate aroma littered with spices and a twist of peel. Delicate spice and peel flavours on the palate are supported by a fine, mealy character and dry, refreshing attitude. Lovely thirst quencher, a little lean. Satisfying, crisp.

7

BAROONA ORIGINAL

Deep brassy gold with a steep, close, creamy head and a dazzle of orange laced citrus aroma on the nose. There is malt too, deep, clear, slightly mealy aromas that give complexity and impact. Malt on the palate is also precise, crisp and deep, adding lithe texture to the slight grumble of bitter hops that builds nicely to a long, dry, malt warmed finish. Very fine beer, tasty, stylish, firm.

9

BAROONA DARK ALE

Deep, dark, brown hued amber with a loose, creamy rich head the colour of latté. Classy bouquet has a delightful fragrance about it, but is otherwise deep and toast tinged, with hints of marmite, currants, chocolate fudge and minerals. Good texture and palate weight give a creamy, almost silky feel to the deep flavours that have more toast, marmite and currants in their complexity and an edge of ripe bitterness. Ripe tasting beer, dry and very long. Another beauty.

BAROONA FEST BIER

Brassy gold with a delicious looking steep, creamy, close packed head. Bouquet is orangey with a delicate hint of spice and some rather succulent malt characters. The palate has more orange and a big, clear malt hit that has a soft, mildly creamy dimension and deep, fresh baked biscuit warmth. Flavour depth is excellent and there are nice floral hop notes right through, coming with a rush at the finish which is long, trimmed with malt sweetness and riding on brisk, mellow astringency. Top beer.

BAROONA FULL MALTY

Very attractive beer, deep, brown hued amber with red highlights and a fine head. Finesse is obvious on the nose too, which is floral and spicy over deeply aromatic malt aromas that have complexity and presence. Complex, soft palate is rich and full, yet cleverly balanced so that it has a sense of elegance as well as power. Overall subtle sweetness is always contained by malt flavour and enough dryness to keep it interesting. Very sophisticated, finely tuned, scrumptious beer.

KAHIKATEA
BREWERY

Address 256 Kahikatea Drive, Hamilton

Phone 07 847 0705

Available for tastings Yes

Opening hours 2pm – 6pm, Tuesday – Friday; 12pm – 6pm, Saturday

Tours Yes, by arrangement

This mid-sized producer is the last survivor of Hamilton's relatively long history of brewing, established in 1995. It has quickly gained good support in the Waikato region, where it provides styles similar to those that have dominated New Zealand brewing for the past century.

KAHIKATEA GOLD

Light gold with a good head and a hoppy, leafy bouquet. Hoppy notes on the palate too, which has a good measure of slightly creamy textured malt, leafiness and a mild, sweet finish. Tasty, attractive beer.

5 | 10

KAHIKATEA DRAUGHT

Dark amber coloured beer with a full head and brisk bouquet with citrus and slight mint aromas, with just a dash of marmite amongst the ripe malty notes. The palate is all malt, slightly sweet, suave, and rather simple after such a brassy introduction.

4 | 10

KAHIKATEA BITTER

Copper amber, with a very malty nose that has hints of crème caramel and a slight frisk of floral/leafy hops. Malty flavours tend to nuts, with a tight, firm texture and a finish that is both sweet and dry with a mild, lingering astringency.

3 | 10

KAHIKATEA DARK

Dark, deep, copper tinged beer with a very rich malt aroma that is slightly roasted and simple, with a hint of chocolate at the end. The palate is light, malt driven and pretty, with chocolate, roasted nuts, mild toast and other dark malt characters all gently understated. A charmer.

WHITE CLIFFS
BREWING CO.

Address RD 44 Main North Rd, SH3, Urenui, Taranaki

Phone 06 752 3676, 0508 4 MIKES (0508 4 64537)

Website www.brewing.co.nz/mikes.htm

Available for tastings Yes

Opening hours 10am – 6pm, 7 days

Tours Yes, by arrangement

If any of the new breweries is an institution, Mike's is. He makes one beer, his way, a style that is unique and finely crafted with honesty and a simple certainty that is most rewarding – if you like Mike's Mild Ale. If you don't, you probably don't like beer at all.

Get it direct by one of the most efficient mail order operators in the country, all the way from Taranaki. Why every pub from Waitara to Wanganui doesn't stock it is a mystery.

MIKE'S MILD ALE

Deep, soft brown/amber with a light, open head. Ripely malty bouquet, pure and clear, suggesting biscuits and grain with a vague fruity note in the distance. Warm, nutty, well conditioned palate with some pleasant hop crunch in the middle and at the end, but really this is all about malt, warm and convivial, from fresh baked biscuits to roasted cashews. An honest beer given a sense of style with a dry, cashew nut finish that lingers romantically.

8 10

SUNSHINE
BREWING CO.

Gisborne will always have a special place in New Zealand beer history because of Gold Top, a lager made by Conrad Breutsch who was brought to the country by Hancock's to make their first lager *Bismark* in 1900. In 1908 Breutsch moved to DJ Barry in Gisborne and created the classic Gold Top.

In that tradition, Sunshine Brewery has regained an important place for Gisborne in New Zealand's brewing culture, quietly getting on with the job of making beers of integrity and character since its first brews were produced in 1989.

Address 109 Disraeli Street, Gisborne

Phone 06 867 7777

Website www.gisbornegold.co.nz

Opening hours 9am – 6pm, Monday – Saturday

Tastings Yes

Tours Yes, by arrangement

BLACK MAGIC STOUT

Deep, dark, light headed, brown coloured ale with a very toasty, burnt nose that is surprisingly understated. Mid weight with nice toasty, roasted nut flavours and a lean texture. Malty finish has a touch of sweetness. Very pleasant, attractive, easy drinking beer.

 5 10

GISBORNE BITTER

Amber, mild, malty beer, easy and soft, with a nicely ripe hop touch to it.

 3 10

GISBORNE GOLD LAGER

Golden coloured, with an open, white head and freshly malty, clean bouquet with a light, mineral-like character.

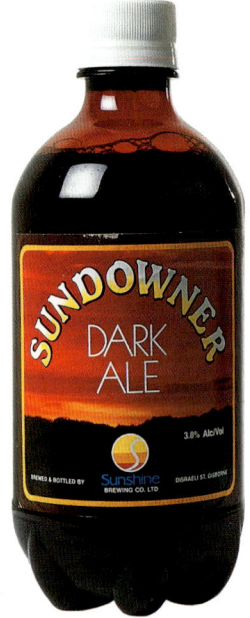

The malty palate is light and crisp, complemented by a moderate hop bitterness and a dash of minerals that give the finish a certain ping to it. Soft, easy, individual beer, with a fresh, lightly malty finish and casual demeanour.

6

SUNDOWNER DARK ALE

Deep, copper-red with a light head and malty, toasty, coffee aromas. Simple palate of toasted malt, sweet feeling but dry finished.

3

FESTIVE LAGER (SPECIAL BREW)

Healthy golden colour with a foamy white head. Ripe malt and hop aroma, spiced with hints of nuts and soy sauce, is most appealing. Flavour is immediately positive, mouth filling, with good weight and depth, malty ripeness and a good hop twist of bitterness. There is a lot going on here, especially in the flavour department, although the texture and balance give an angular impression. Tasty, lingering, dry, assertive beer.

7

LIMBURG
BREWING CO.

High class micro in Hastings where Chris O'Leary has rapidly established a reputation as one of the most talented brewers around, first with a sequence of very smart weiss and wit biers, and latterly with Hopsmacker Pale Ale. Hopsmacker has become something of a rare star amongst beer enthusiasts in the last six months.

Address 500 William St, Hastings

Phone 06 877 0415

Available for tastings Yes

Opening hours 2pm – 6pm, Thursday & Friday; 10am – 4pm, Saturday

Tours Yes, by arrangement

WEISSBIER

Cloudy light amber coloured with a terrific, close, creamy head. The nose is spicy, aromatic, tinged with ripe grain, citrus and plump fruit aromas. Crisp, clean, spicy cereal palate is warm and complex, gently fruity with a light, lingering, surprisingly dry finish. Beautifully crafted, delightful, fine beer.

 8 10

REDCOAT AMBER ALE

Deep, glossy red/amber with a steep, creamy head and a deliciously ripe nose that is full of fruit, tangerine and fragrantly crisp hops. Malty palate has depth and momentum, with cereal aromas to the fore, supported by a faintly herbal hop character that dominates through the end with a vibrant, tasty bitterness over tangerine fruit layers. Good texture provides a suave dimension, balancing hop bitterness with charm. Very classy beer, lighter than it seems at first, but packed with flavour.

 8 10

HOPSMACKER PALE ALE

Steep headed, rich golden/amber coloured beer with a crisp, beautifully floral/citrus bouquet that is fragrant and complex with malt and fruit. Orange and fresh malt palate dances with fruit and a light, brisk malt flavour that runs right through to the long, dry, gently bitter finish. Classy beer, with hop flavour in the middle, good condition and texture, it is fruity, pure and very elegant.

 9 10

WEIZENBOCK

Fat, creamy, latté coloured head on a deep, dark, black-eyed body is almost as inviting as the aromatic, burned toffee bouquet that smells remarkably like Callard and Bowser's best. Rich, deep aromatic fruit complexities on the nose are matched on the palate with almost pineapple fruit, with charred toffee and a lush texture giving sophistication to the sense of power. Long, long flavours fade nicely from mild sweetness to a dry, herb tinged finish and lingering toffee/char. Superb.

 9 10

ALTHEIMER ALTBIER

Deep copper amber with a creamy, close head and deeply malt bouquet that has nuts and sweet hints of butterscotch foremost amongst its aromatic nuances, with a distant hint of floral hops. Ripely malty, slightly nutty palate has fruit and very clean, crisp malt/cereal characters. Classy feeling, precise, crisply nutty beer with a floral wisp of hops.

 7 10

WITBIER

Light, cloudy, amber brown with a steep, lightly creamy head. Fragrant, spicy nose is classically stuffed with orange peel and a background zing of fine cereal, almost like fresh cornflakes. Orangey, spicy palate is light and complex with a fresh, dry finish that lingers on nicely. Clean and lively, refreshing beer.

 7 10

MATES
BREWERY

A mid-sized regional brewery based at Onekawa, Napier.

Hawkes Bay Independent
Brewery (Mates Brewery)

Address 42 Holden Street,
Onekawa, Napier

Phone 06 843 3719

Available for tastings No

Opening hours 8am – 5pm,
Monday – Friday

Tours Yes, by arrangement

MATES DRAUGHT

Amber colour with a soft, malty, slight hop touched
bouquet and very soft, clean, easy going palate.

MATES AMBER

Amber colour with a good head, lightly hopped bouquet
with plenty of clear, clean malt. Malt dominates the palate,
which is mild and soft with a slight dryness at the finish.

MATES LAGER

Bright golden colour, light, fresh, slightly sweet, malty nose
with a distant hop freshness. Palate is crisper, with pure
malt flavours, fresh and lightly sweet. Simple, pleasantly
crisp with a very mild hop touch at the end.

MATES DARK

Deep, dark amber/brown colour with char and toast notes
on the nose, some touches of chocolate and roasted malt.
Very light palate, soft, slightly sweet finishing, clean, nutty/
toasty at the end.

3 10

ROOSTERS
BREWHOUSE

Micro established on the western edge of Hastings in Hawkes Bay, with the intention of making "traditional, natural batch brewed beer for the rural working man." The convivial roadside establishment is well worth a stop if you are wandering in the region, especially at the end of the working day when it fills up with locals.

Address 1470 Omahu Road, Hastings

Phone 06 879 4127

Available for tastings Yes

Opening hours 10am – 7pm, Monday – Saturday

Tours Yes, by arrangement

ROOSTERS HAYMAKER

Polished, golden brass coloured beer with a good, white head and ripely malty, citrus-flecked bouquet that is rather reserved in spite of its gentle charm, with a mineral edge giving it a sort of muscular nature. The palate is big yet mildly flavoured, very malty, biscuits and lightly roasted nuts, even grainy at times, with a slight astringency at the finish. Very clear and precise, with a muscular nature throughout. Not for the fainthearted.

6 10

ROOSTERS LAGER

Golden coloured beer with a clean white head and an aroma that is neatly balanced between clear malt and a leafy hoppiness. Flavour has the same balance of character, in part hop astringency that is positive and grainy, on the other hand sweetly malty, clear and pure. Quite refreshing, especially with its dry, almost astringent finish. A definite style.

7 10

ROOSTERS DARK ALE

Deep amber with a brown touch and a slight fruit lift on the essentially nutty, toasty bouquet that is only mildly aromatic. Pleasant weight of flavour and continuation of the nutty, very mildly fruity character, it finishes surprisingly light, with a passing nuttiness and gentle dry touch.

 5 10

ROOSTERS GOLDEN WHEAT

Wheat beer with balls, in spite of what seems on the surface a rather delicate nature; pale in colour, lightly aromatic with just a twist of spice and sweetly malty mildness. Malty, sweetly nutty palate with a lisp of honey and some soft, sweet spice at the finish that lingers beautifully, supported by a staunch, warm nature that could cut you down very quickly if you aren't careful.

 6 10

ROOSTERS DRAUGHT

Amber with a pretty head and a malty, lightly nutty bouquet. Soft, malty palate has an appealing freshness and clean, pure biscuit character. Soft finishing, pleasant beer.

 4 10

TUI
BREWERY

Architecturally one of the finest breweries in the country, it has been the largest business in the tiny Wairarapa township of Mangatainoka virtually since it was established in 1889. It has also been a significant feature in the social life of the southern part of the North Island as a major regional beer brand for more than a century.

Since it was taken over by DB in 1969 it has gained more national recognition, and in recent years has become something of a *brand célèbre* amongst students in all the university cities.

All the beers here, Tui as well as the mainstream DB range, are made by continuous fermentation.

Address Main Road, Mangatainoka, Pahiatua

Phone 06 376 7549

Available for tastings No

Opening hours 9am – 1pm, Monday – Friday

Tours 10.30am and 1pm daily, bookings essential

TUI EAST INDIA PALE ALE

Nothing like the beer style it claims to be, but a pleasant, copper coloured, aromatic beer with a tinge of florid yeast and light malt in its bouquet, and a soft, mealy, malty palate with a sweet finish. Nicely creamy texture helps make this an easy drinking charmer.

3 | 10

SHAMROCK
BREWING CO.

Small brewery offering a local alternative to the big brands.

Address 267 Main Street, Palmerston North

Phone 06 355 2130

Available for tastings Yes

Opening hours 10am 'til late, 7 days

Tours Yes, by arrangement

SHAMROCK LAGER

Golden colour, soft, malty, slight florid yeast bouquet and a mild, malty, slightly sweet palate. Gentle, pleasant beer.

SHAMROCK STRONG

Deep amber/brown with a toast, roasty bouquet that is very malty and faintly astringent. Sweet, roasted palate is re-markably light and soft after the pushy aroma, and the finish light and soft.

SHAMROCK DRAUGHT

Ripe colour is amber/brown with a beige head of nice texture. Bouquet is soft and very mellow, with a slight aroma of dainty malt. The palate is similar, soft and simple, sweet.

SHAMROCK STOUT

Black-hearted deep amber with brown lights, and a strong burned aroma that is part toast, part nuts and very em-phatic, with just a dash of molasses/malt extract at the end. The palate is very light after this, soft, charred and short.

KATIPO
BREWING CO.

Originally began operations as Valley Brewing Company in the old Lower Hutt railway station in 1991. The station had been renovated as a brewpub, known as the Parrot and Jigger, at the heart of the Station Village development in Lower Hutt, which continues to provide a home for the Katipo Brewing Co. beers.

Address Station Village, 499 Hutt Road, Lower Hutt

Phone 04 939 1040

Available for tastings Yes

Opening hours 11am 'til late, Monday – Sunday

Tours Yes, by arrangement

KATIPO DRAUGHT

Steep, light creamy coloured head on golden amber beer with a lightly aromatic bouquet with dramatic, orangey fruit and fresh, warm malt characters. Very easy going texture and a light, crisp, malty palate with real delicacy and fine malt flavours mingled with fruit. Dry, clean, charming beer.

7 10

KATIPO PALE ALE

Ripe golden colour with a good head and lightly fruity, citrus-tinged bouquet that is filled with round, soft, clear malt notes. Excellent hops on the palate give grit and momentum to the delicious malty flavours that slide nicely to the finish with a suave smoothness that ends dry, faintly leafy, with a touch of astringency. Light and flavourful, elegant, deep, smart as beer.

8 10

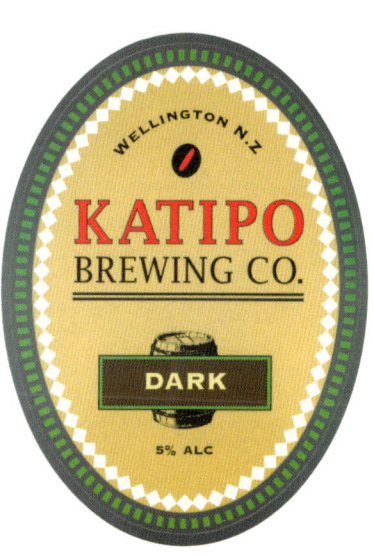

KATIPO DARK

Deep brown/amber with a fragrant, fruity nose showing plenty of Vogel's toast with a slight dab of liquorice, pure cereal malt and mild nuttiness. Deep flavoured mid palate has more nuts and slight fruit, with liquorice and warmth at the very end, where dry, slightly leafy hops give it a neat flick of astringency. Delicious, sophisticated dark beer with poise and panache.

 8 10

KATIPO STRONG ALE

Deep, brassy amber with a very close, tight head and fruity, banana flecked bouquet alive with lashings of clear, bright malt. Very malty, fruity, soft palate has warmth and strength as well as clear, Jersey Caramel-like malt sweetness, svelte texture and subtle, just enough to be interesting, hop character. Long, warm and very suave.

 8 10

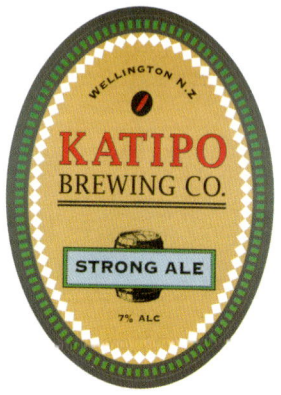

KATIPO SPECIAL STOUT

Dark, deep amber brown with a crisply mellow, fine toasted Vogel's nose that also has toffee and orange characters. Soft, creamy textured, deeply flavoured beer with hints of fruit and some lovely hop astringency to keep the balance, it slides off to a charred nuttiness that is softened by chocolate flavours and refreshed with a tang of hop astringency. Fine craft.

 8 10

McCASHIN'S
BREWERY & MALTHOUSE

The first independent to open in New Zealand for half a century when it began brewing in Stoke in 1981, Mac's not only signalled a return to all malt beer, it revived interest in the craft of brewing. The result is found not just in the range of Mac's beer, but in an active, high quality craft brewing community in Nelson and Marlborough. Mac's is now wholly owned by Lion, although the Nelson brewery continues to operate much as it has since it began.

Address 660 Main Road, Stoke, Nelson

Phone 03 547 0526

Website www.macsbeer.co.nz

Available for tastings Yes

Opening hours 9.30am – 6pm, Monday – Saturday; 10am – 4pm, Sunday

Tours 11am and 2pm or by prior arrangement

MAC'S GOLD

Light yellow/gold coloured beer with a close, white head. Softly aromatic with sweet malt and a light touch of hops. Clean, soft malt palate, very easy, with a subtle dash of mid palate hops that keeps the sweetness in check, just. Clean, light finish.

 5 10

MAC'S COPPERHOP

Copper/amber colour with a reddish hue and softly creamy head. Bouquet is flamboyantly exotic, dancing with ripe citrus aromas and a deep, lush old-rose richness that is quite remarkable. There are some quite sweet, clear malt tones under all this hoppy extravagance, if you care to look, and malt ripeness too, on the palate, which is crisp and beautifully balanced. Very slick, suave textured with moderate mid palate hops and a real, toothsome astringency of floral hops at the end. Flavourful, finely crafted beer with character and panache. If this is what the major breweries can do, New Zealand beer has a dazzling future.

9 10

MAC'S NELSON RESERVE PREMIUM LAGER

Good, strong head on a light, golden brass coloured body with a delightfully citric hop bouquet that is clean and fresh, mellowed by a crisp, pure malt note. Strong palate is well flavoured, dry, balanced and precise, with hop astringency in the middle and at the finish, which is long and shapely. Smart beer, deftly made.

 7 10

MAC'S REAL ALE

Bright amber with a close, creamy head. Light malt/toffee cream nose, with vague fruit but otherwise lager in style. Light, round, soft palate, easy and short, gently malty, clean.

 3 10

MAC'S LIGHT

Yellow/gold with a light head and a soft, malty nose with a touch of light malt. Malt palate is also light, clean and fresh.

 2 10

BLACK MAC

Deep, dark amber, with a creamy, close head. Light nose is slightly nutty, unusually fresh, with a distinct toasted character and a measure of soft chocolate. Toasted Vogel's palate has nutty aspects and a light feel that has a twist of astringency at the finish. Soft chocolate and nutty notes add interest. Conservative, mellow beer.

 5 10

THE MUSSEL INN
BREWPUB

Legendary at the top of the South Island, this remarkable establishment deserves to be a national symbol of how good hospitality can be in this country if we play to our strengths. Idyllically located at Onekaka, Golden Bay, half way between Takaka and Collingwood, this roadside pub cum café is as much a haven of conviviality and good music as of fine beverages and hearty food. What is more, the food and drink are an emphatic celebration of character and regional individuality.

All the wines, ciders and soft drinks are produced on site, as well as the beer, which is a tour de force of brewing virtuosity. The only disappointment is that you have to travel all the way to Golden Bay to try beers that are already New Zealand classics. Then again, even if you don't drink beer, it is well worth the trip.

An interesting feature of the beers is their names, which make the collection sound like a menagerie, from Monkey Puzzle to Pale Whale Ale. The idea is that in a noisy, crowded bar there is no need for verbal beer orders, simple sign language overcomes any communication problems. As you read the tasting notes below, imagine the performance required to order each in a noisy bar. Even on a quiet Sunday it was rather disconcerting to hear a local come up to the bar and order, "Two horses, a goose, an ox and a whale, thanks."

Andrew Dixon began brewing here in 1995, with the job now in the hands of Reuben Lee. The culture is organic, the beers are as elegant as anywhere. Let's hope they go on forever. ·

Address Onekaka, RD 2, Takaka

Phone 03 525 9241

Website www.musselinn.co.nz

Available for tastings Yes, by arrangement

Opening hours 11am 'til late, 7 days

Tours Yes, by arrangement

GOLDEN GOOSE LAGER

Golden yellow/brass with a fine head and delicate, subtle citrus hop aroma over a buttery malt heart. Round, crisp, malty palate with a clean, fresh finish, well conditioned and completed with a twist of hop astringency that keeps it interesting. Well made, nicely balanced, satisfying beer.

 7 10

CAPTAIN COOKER MANUKA BEER

Soft, lightly creamy head on a copper amber body and a big, orange peel nose with fragrant rose hints and a coffee backnote. Complex, abundant and unique, it is an especially inviting introduction to a beer with a big Vienna-like palate, dry with a soft, creamy texture and nutty malt flavour, a hint of coffee, finely tuned with astringency and floral/herbal tones that give a brisk edge to the lingering, flavourful finish. Very complex, there are fruit and flowers, toffee and spice in here, delivered with balance and elegance that always invites another taste. Flavoured *à la* Captain Cook with manuka tips alongside a good measure of hops, this is a New Zealand classic. Great stuff.

 10 10

PALE WHALE ALE

Light golden brass with an open head and beautiful, aromatic bouquet laced with hop notes that evoke spicy roses and limes, with a base of mellow malt. Slight toffee flavour on the palate, which is suave textured and brightened by a frisky hop character and a consistent citrus note that lasts well into the finish. Finishes dry with a mild astringency and crisp, malty/spicy flavour that lasts and lasts. Super beer, well flavoured but never pushy, it is all elegance and deft detail.

 8 10

HEAT RASH CHILLI BEER

A burning novelty from the moment the bright red cayenne chilli pepper pops out of the bottle into your glass, where it floats aggressively in the light head. Aromatic, red capsicum nose is assertive, moderated by light malt and a vaguely herbal hop note. Good malt flavour is seared by chilli heat and capsicum flavours that are somehow in harmony with herbal hops and slick malt that give it momentum and flavour length as well as lingering heat. The blend of cool beer and chilli fire is intriguing, and probably addictive. The beer is a blast. Only in bottles, and no two are the same, as it depends on the length of time the chilli has been trapped and each chilli pepper's particular mood.

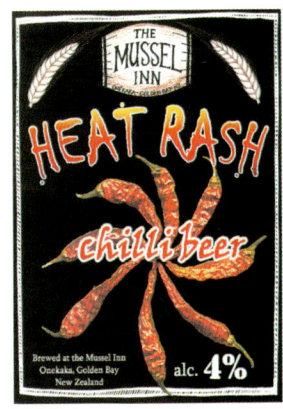

 9 10

RED HERRING SMOKEY BEER

Glowing, creamy white head on a copper amber body introduces a fragrant, smokey, slightly edgy-smelling beer with an earthy quality. Tastes of smoke and earth, too, with a brisk texture and nutty malt base. Quite suave and nicely detailed with a clever counterbalance of smoke and hop astringency at the finish which keeps up your interest. Elegant beer, with enough malt clarity and hop zing to keep the smoke in balance.

 8 10

WHISKY KISS BOURBON BARREL FERMENTED

A fun park beer with the vociferous, vanilla primed aroma of American oak kept tidy by a sneeze of citrus hops. Quite astringent right through, with vanilla tones, a bristle of hop and a strange, pervasive sweetness that is only just controlled by the hop zest. Austere, astringent finish has plenty of flavour and some interesting details.

 6 10

STRONG OX

Deep, dark, blackish amber topped by a light coffee crema head. Fragrant, deep Jaffa aroma, orange and chocolate with details of roasted nuts and malt biscuits. Very suave, soft but virile palate is perfectly pitched with fruity aspects, more orange and chocolate, and a balancing hops blues, a slightly gravelly richness of texture that is especially sexy. Big beer, yet detailed and superbly balanced into a class act.

 9 10

DARK HORSE STOUT

Superb, creamy head on a deep, darkly coloured beer that has a surprisingly delicate, aromatic bouquet, a citrus touched harmony of coffee, toast, and chocolate aromas. Impact is fine and well hopped, with an undercurrent of soft richness, Vogel's toast flavours and nuances of coffee, with an ever-present hoppiness that gives it a brisk dimension, and long, lingering, light finish. Very individual, perfectly balanced stout with a light touch.

 7 10

MONKEY PUZZLE

Copper amber beer with a pretty, tinted, close head and lightly fragrant bouquet, sprinkled with spicy orange and rose petal aromas and a dusty, light sweetness. Lovely palate, big and warm yet delicately balanced, spicy, with a touch of sweetness and a lacy complex of flavour. Very long, astringent, orange-tinged finish. This is seriously big beer that manages to be poised as well as powerful. Easy to love it, easy to fall over doing so.

 8 10

LIGHTHOUSE
BREWERY

Dick Tout has made the transition from home brewer to professional with style, and his tiny Nelson brewery not only makes some of the classiest beers around, his distinctive blue and white label is simply the best in the country. Named after Nelson's historic lighthouse, Tout began the business in 1996. While this is the smallest legal brewery in the country, it is hard to imagine why every proud Nelson beer drinker is not demanding an increase in production.

Address 280 Hardy St, Nelson

Phone 03 548 8983

Available for tastings Yes, by arrangement

Opening hours 9.30am – 5pm, Monday – Friday; closed Tuesday afternoon; 9.30am – 12.30pm, Saturday

Tours Yes, by arrangement

TASMAN BAY PILSNER

Yellow gold with a light, clean head. Sweetly aromatic hop nose with a clean malt note, fresh and bright with a citrus note and a mildly creamy/funky character. Big, crisp palate, full of aromatic hop flavours and bristly textures, lean and dry, with a mineral note at the finish and a touch of creaminess. Perfect, crisp, well-shaped, lingering, tasting beer with a firm, herbal hop end. All class.

 9 | 10

DICK'S DARK

Deep amber brown with a light, beige head. Roasted, mellow malt bouquet, soft and floral/fruity with a hint of roasted nuts and chocolate. Floral hops in the first mouthful, too, with a ripe, roasted mid palate that has depth and texture as well as moderate weight and a frisk of hops. Lovely balance and condition, with a sense of being a deep, mild ale, with an excellent dry, hoppy, chocolate fringed finish. Delicious beer, beautifully crafted.

 8 | 10

CLASSIC STOUT

Deep, dark black with a fine coffee crema head and a ripe bouquet laced with coffee and chocolate and burned Vogel's toast aromas, a dash of fruit and a tang of green hops in the background. Toasty, ripe palate is also touched with a dash of hop herbals that give it a dry character, gently rich and very long. Has full, well-shaped flavours with hints of chocolate and toast to the very end. Classy stuff.

8 **10**

HAULASHORE BITTER

Light head on a golden copper beer with fragrant, floral hops aromas nudged by fruity notes, a slight green tang that is almost minty and clear, crisp malt. Impact of hop frisked, malt pure character leads to a firmly flavoured, well weighted mid palate that is supported by strong hop characters and inviting astringency. Big flavoured, firm beer with a long, dry, hoppy finish.

7 **10**

FOUNDERS
BREWERY

Appropriately this micro is located in Founders Historic Park in Nelson, a museum settlement of historic buildings and replicas from Nelson's brewery-rich colonial days. The beer matches the historic importance of the site, too, organic brews made with the sort of craft that once inspired loyal support for local beer. A must stop for visitors to Nelson, a beer for locals to be proud of.

Address Founders Historic Park, 87 Atawhai Drive, Nelson

Phone 03 548 4638

Website www.biobrew.co.nz

Available for tastings Yes

Opening hours 10am – 4.30pm, 7 days (Summer only)

Tours Yes, by arrangement

TALL BLONDE

Yellow gold beer with a fine collar of white. Fresh, citrus fragrant, lightly malty bouquet with substance and a crisp nature. Plump malt palate with a quite succulent middle, the Saaz hop presence throughout is impressive, uplifting, always refreshing. Clean, crisp, well-balanced beer, slightly soft at the finish, with a citrus tang.

 7 10

REDHEAD

Deep copper coloured beer with an attractive, creamy looking, cream coloured head. Very inviting. Its big, citrus Saaz hop nose makes it emphatically local, with a frisky edge and some delicious mellow tones of nutty, soft, malt that has a rich shortbread quality. Big-flavoured, ripe, hop-laced palate has astringency and suave texture in lively balance, with a creamy mid-palate, complex, touched with mineral characters and very long. Terrific beer.

 8 10

LONG BLACK

Dark, deep, black-hued amber with a light, coffee crema
head and big, dark aroma jammed with roasted nuts,
honey and toasted Vogel's, with just a slight burr of chocolate. Surprisingly fresh palate, light, crisp and clean with
layers of plump chocolate and roasted nut malt fading off
in a toasty finish. Light, charming black beer.

NELSON BAYS
BREWERY

Established in 1993 to supply Nelson district's clubs and pubs with an alternative to Mac's and the mainstream beer suppliers, Nelson Bays has developed as a supplier of standard New Zealand industrial beer styles. The emergence of Exclamator Doppelbock, however, not only marks a new direction for a company with a very talented brewer, but a tasty alternative for its supporters.

Address 89 Pascoe St, Tahunanui, Nelson

Phone 03 547 8097, 0800 833 007

Website www.baysbrewery.co.nz

Available for tastings Yes

Opening hours 8am – 5.30pm, Monday – Thursday; 8am – 6pm, Friday; 11am – 6pm, Saturday; 12.30am – 5pm, Sunday

Tours Yes, by arrangement

BAYS GOLD LAGER

Yellow gold with a tall, close white head. Fresh, lightly citrus toned malty bouquet, pleasant and lightly sweet. Palate is crisp, malty, with a light, clear malt sweetness and just a fringe of citrus/green malt. Fresh, light finish. Pleasant, mellow beer.

 4 10

EXCLAMATOR NELSON DOPPELBOCK

Creamy head is close and pale in colour, nicely contrasting with the rich, copper amber colour beneath. Fragrant/aromatic lift on the nose is gently fruity, with a dash of floral hops and rich malt biscuit notes, simultaneously inviting and satisfying. Palate has lovely texture from the first hit, creamy, almost glossy, with light toast flavours and a fresh, orange-like tang, complemented by some gravelly hop growl that winds up in a long, toasty, fruit and dryly astringent finish. Ripe beer, lovely to drink with its balance of sweet and dry, rich and astringent. More please.

 7 10

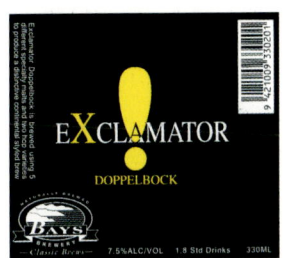

BAYS DRAUGHT ALE

Light, copper amber with a close, tight head. Malty nose, biscuity and gently sweet with a light tang of yeast and some butterscotch notes. Soft, creamy malt palate is sweet and light with an easy malty finish. Very tidy.

 3 10

BAYS DARK ALE

Light coffee cream head on a deep, darkly amber beer. Toasty Vogel's nose is typical and appealing, with some nuts and a light chocolate hint. Soft texture is mild, sweet, and toasty with a light toasty finish. Very mellow, soft, gentle beer.

 3 10

HARRINGTON'S

BREWERY, NELSON

The Nelson twin of Harrington's in Christchurch, they share some of the same beers, while others are exclusive to each, resulting in a double tasting of some of the beers. The notes below are as tasted from each location. Both establishments have a tradition that stretches back deep into New Zealand's brewing history, and both have established a significant place in the brewing renaissance of their particular regions.

Address 53 Beach Road, Richmond, Nelson

Phone 03 544 8675

Website www.harringtonsbrewery.co.nz

Available for tastings Yes

Opening hours 10am – 6pm, Monday – Saturday

Tours Yes, by arrangement

HARRINGTON'S WHEAT BEER

Light, pretty gold. Malty, mildly spicy aroma with a delicately spiced palate, softly malty with a crisp, pleasantly dry finish.

 4 10

HARRINGTON'S BOULDER BANK LAGER

Attractive gold colour with a crisp open textured, white head. Very mild bouquet, fine and malty with a dash of herbal hops and a hint of spice. Clean, crisp palate, very light, dry and ripely malty at the finish. Soft in style, light, pretty.

 4 10

HARRINGTON'S TASMAN LAGER

Ripe golden colour with a light, white, loose head and a mildly hoppy aroma that is part herbs, part dried flowers with a dash of citrus and a sweet malt character. Positive, fresh palate, with brisk, green hop characters over some pure light malt. Flavourful, crisp and with enough astringency to give it a lively demeanour, and a lingering, green herb, dry finish. Direct, no nonsense beer.

 6 | 10

HARRINGTON'S BEST BITTER

Pure amber, bright and clean with a gentle head and a lovely malty aroma trimmed with hops that smells especially lagerish. Malty/nutty impact introduces a palate that is positive, flavourful and very clean, precise, with a neat measure of hops and lovely balance between astringency, sweet malt and nutty, mealy, even coffee-tinged, flavour. Has lovely weight and balance, with a mouthful of flavour and positive finish. A beauty.

 8 | 10

HARRINGTON'S FINEST LAGER

Pretty gold with an open, fresh white head. Delightful hop aroma is slightly citrus, slightly floral, backed by a warm dash of malt and an unusual fruitness. Clean, fresh palate is full of malt, with a herbal hop background and a long, hop tinged finish. Dry and lingering, its crisp edge most refreshing, has nice balance and delicacy.

 6 | 10

HARRINGTON'S CANTERBURY PALE ALE

Light copper/amber, with a frothy white head. Bouquet is aromatic with hops, dry and brisk, just a tinge citric, mostly floral, and faintly fruity, with a chunk of fresh malt sweetness. Light, tasty palate has plenty of hop feel, but less flavour, with the malt filling in any gaps and the hops giving lively appeal. A lighter version, not really an ale in character, but crisp and sure and delightfully hop filled, all the way to its dry finish, it is really a meaty lager, and a good one.

| 7 | 10 |

HARRINGTON'S BOULDER BANK PREMIUM DRAUGHT

Copperish amber with a light, open head. Soft, malty nose, simple. Light, malty, pleasant palate. Clean and simple.

| 3 | 10 |

HARRINGTON'S BOULDER BANK PREMIUM DARK

Deep, very dark, amber hued with an open, coffee cream head. Simple, very toasty bouquet with a trace of molasses and marmite intensity. Light, toasty flavour impact is followed by some chocolate hints that build and deliver a charming chocolate soft finish that lingers nicely. Light-weight dark beer, well balanced, soft and fresh, with pretty flavours.

| 6 | 10 |

HARRINGTON'S WOBBLY BOOT DARK ALE

Deep, dark amber with a black heart and a lovely, soft looking cafe crema head. Surprisingly subtle bouquet, deep with toasty, nutty, chocolate notes, a light fruit quality and pervasive softness. Ripe, mouthfilling impact of soft, suave, deep flavours with hints of Afghan biscuits, a fruit suggestion and a mellow, charming, lingering darkness of character that is neither sweet nor dry. A warm, cuddly, convivial beer.

| 7 | 10 |

HARRINGTON'S STOUT

Black dark with a brown hint and cafe crema coloured head. Toasty, smoke tinged bouquet is deep and hard edged, mineral-like. Big, tasty palate has toast, smoke and charred nuts with a hop presence that builds towards the end delivering an astringent twist that matches the minerals and rich, deep flavours. Quite charred at the finish, it lingers nicely, quite fresh and dry. Smart stuff.

6 10

DODSON'S
MARLBOROUGH BREWERY

Dodson's first began life as the Wairau Brewery in 1858 as the Marlborough branch of Nelson's already established brewing dynasty. After failing under the pressures of prohibition, the name has been revived by Marlborough Brewery, a company formed by local pub owners a decade ago to give them a competitive edge over the big two. Renamed Dodson's in 2002, it has reclaimed the old Dodson's brewery and malthouse in Blenheim, which have been both ice cream factory and winery before being returned to the brewing fold. The malthouse has been converted into a rather smart bar and restaurant, and the brewery is showing increasing interest in handcrafted beers of real interest.

Address 1 Dodson St, Blenheim

Phone 03 577 8348

Available for tastings Yes

Opening hours 11am 'til late, 7 days

Tours Yes, by arrangement

DODSON'S SPECIAL LAGER

Bright brass gold, loose head. Strong malty/hoppy bouquet, aromatic with dry, slightly citrus flower hops and toffeeish malt. Malt/yeast palate with light hop middle, yeast is a tad florid. Slight sourness at finish, short, not dry. Pleasant.

 3 10

DODSON'S PILSNER

Bright yellow brass. Floral bouquet with a pungent, herbal hop note and sweet malt background. Flavoursome middle, with a clean edge, ripe, mealy/creamy mid-palate with a long, herbal, fresh finish. Clean and deliciously mellowed with a complex kick.

 7 10

DODSON'S DRAUGHT

Deep copper/amber with a good, open head. Aromatic, toasty bouquet with a hint of caramel/toffee and a flick of hop florals. Toasty/smoky firm mid palate, slightly nutty with excellent flavour length. Quite unique, a sort of lightweight black beer style. Light, well balanced, crisp and tasty.

 5 **10**

MARLBOROUGH RED DEVIL

Good head, copper brass colour. Quite nutty, aromatic malt bouquet, mild hops. Soft, light malty palate, clean, pleasant, with a delicate citric nudge at the end.

 4 **10**

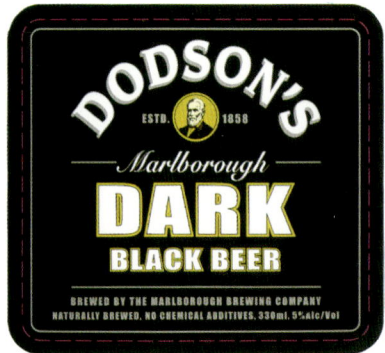

DODSON'S STEAM

Ripe red amber with a light, close head, very attractive looking. Rich, malty bouquet with toast and a citrus hop tang amongst the toffee notes. Delicious caramel crème palate, malty, mellow flavours, clean, moderate length beer, mild and delicious dry finish. The hop touch keeps it interesting.

 6 **10**

DODSON'S DARK BLACK BEER

Deep, dark amber with coffee crème coloured, close head. Fine hop aroma leads the bouquet which is chocolate and toast filled, not too assertive, but with substance. Good deep flavour impact, with the char and richness coming up through the middle and a surprisingly fresh, crisp texture and freshness. Very well-balanced, with good weight, but most important and impressive flavour momentum. Finish is a deft touch, giving it a sense of poise. Smart beer.

 8 **10**

PINK ELEPHANT
BREWERY

In the short history of BAT (Beer after Teetotalitariansim) in New Zealand, Roger Pink has already claimed his particularly individual place. Pink is English, so he grew up with bitter and pale ale in his genes, with a pub called The Elephant on the corner of his street. When he grew up he left England and settled in Nelson, with every intention of converting the local beer barbarians into ardent supporters of the English brewing style he was so gallantly introducing to this Pacific backwater.

Nelson had its own ideas about beer, and so Marlborough became the site of the Pink Elephant Brewery and a home for some of the most striking beers and ales that New Zealand has seen. The Pink Elephant is small, its beers emphatically crafted into beer lovers' delights, with reputations unrestrained by boundaries – of any sort.

Address RD 3, Blenheim

Phone 03 572 9467

Available for tastings No

Opening hours Not open to public

Tours Only by prior arrangement

GOLDEN TUSK PBA

Deep, golden brass colour with a big, green hop nose, rich and powerful, tinged with light, toffeeish malt. Toffee, butterscotch notes on the palate with a nice degree of suave texture and a longish, dry finish, with hop presence all through, slightly green, gently abrasive. Mellow, well balanced beer with plenty of interest.

RAJAH

Deep, dark brown/amber with a soft head and a ripe, chocolaty nose with layers of nuts and toast with a dash of fruit. Fruit on the palate too, from first impact right through, attended by nutty, ripe malt characters, some floral hop notes and a sweet, tangy finish. Very fine beer, with excellent balance and weight, giving it momentum and a sense of elegance.

 9 | 10

PDA

Deep, dark beer with a brownish hue in its amber depths. Nose is aromatically hoppy, floral with nuances of green and citrus fruit notes with a softly malty background and warm character. Flavourful palate has more hop presence, with full malt flavours and a dry, hop impregnated finish that is long and satisfying. Very suave beer, with a light, creamy feel given frisk by the hops, poise by the brewer's craft. Stylish and generous.

8 | 10

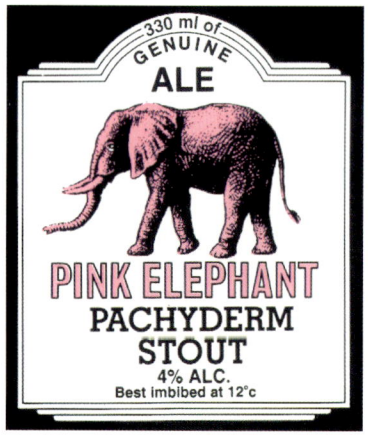

PACHYDERM STOUT

Deep, blackish, dense coloured beer with a dark cream head. Deep, chocolate toast bouquet with a light, floral hop note and some nutty asides. Strong roasted flavours lead to a nutty, hop scorched, malt rich mid palate that has toast and nut details, and a rising hop presence that really asserts itself at the finish, leaving a long, dry, vaguely smoky aftertaste. For all its flavour it has a light, fresh air to it.

 8 | 10

ROGER'S RESERVE

Brass amber with an open, healthy head and big, aromatic bouquet stuffed with orange peel, fruit and a green cut. A real show-off beer, it virtually jumps into your mouth, all orangey and fresh, with lashings of hops and ripe, biscuity malt, but the balance is so fine it leaves a sense of grace with its slightly astringent, hop smeared finish. Very smart, unequivocal beer.

MAMMOTH

Deep, caramel amber colour and an equally deep bouquet, but fine to the point of being fragrant, with floral touches amongst the fruit, a dash of banana, some citrus. Deep, powerful palate has suave texture, with flashes of hop character right through, fruity, toffee-tinged, grainy and quite forceful at the finish. Big beer, crammed with interesting flavours.

MCELLIES

Deep amber with red lights, with a fine, light head and a buttery/banana nose with some nutty, Vogel's toast characters. Mild, clear malt palate with a butterscotch savour, gently soft texture brushed with light astringency and long, warm, muscular finish that is slightly sweet, with a drying aftertaste.

MOTHER'S BRUIN

Deep brown colour and an aromatic, fruity, char edged bouquet that is very deep, sweet with honeyed butterscotch, slightly faded at the edges. Big beer, with nuts and toffee palate, and a honey character that is quite pronounced at the finish. Strong, strangely gentle, it fades quietly away.

TRUMPET

Deep, golden colour with brown hues and a very fine, deeply malty, sweetly aromatic bouquet with a dry trim that is vaguely floral. Ripe malt and wild spice flavours fill the glowing, slick palate that has warmth and breadth enough to warn beginners that this is powerful stuff. The flavour of Jersey Caramel lollies keeps pushing forward through hints of raisins and orange peel, and the finish is round and warm, with just a flick of dryness at the very end.

CANTERBURY
BREWERY

All that remains of Canterbury's long tradition of brewing, and its key role in New Zealand beer as a long time source of quality barley, is this manufactured brand. A division of Lion-Nathan, its signage permeates the upper South Island in an ugly pastiche of regionalism.

CANTERBURY DRAUGHT

Light copper amber. Very light, mild, gently malty nose, with a touch of yeast/ferment character. Soft, malty, light, dry finish.

Address 36 St Asaph St, Christchurch

Phone 03 379 4940

Website www.lion.co.nz

Available for tastings No

Opening hours 9am–5pm, Monday–Friday

Tours 10am and 12.30pm, Monday, Tuesday, Wednesday; Thursday & Friday; 1pm, Saturday; group bookings by arrangement

DUX DE LUX
BREWERY

Brewpub in the middle of Christchurch's old university complex close to the city centre. Began brewing in 1989. Makes 'Free Range' beers in 1200 litre batches. Most beers are brewed with imported malts and hops.

Address Arts Centre, Cnr Hereford & Montreal Streets, Christchurch

Phone 03 366 6919

Website www.thedux.co.nz

Available for tastings Yes, by arrangement

Opening hours 11.30am – 11pm (11.30pm on Friday & Saturday)

Tours Yes, by arrangement

BLACK SHAG STOUT

Dense, burnt, murky bouquet with strong burnt, toasty characters and a nicely trim, hop dried finish. Creamy textured in the middle and some interesting flavour complexities make for a tasty, unusual beer.

 4 | 10

BLUEBERRY BROWN

Plump, fruity, spicy smelling beer with some sweet malt charm. Fruit and spice on the palate, too, along with a mellow, malt sweetness and biscuit flavour. A short, tangy, slightly sour and unusual finish spoils a good start.

 2 | 10

BLUE DUCK DRAUGHT

Amber with a light head and light, slightly sweet, malty nose that has a sour yeast character. Mid weight, with a mild dose of hops coming through in the middle and end. Pleasant.

 3 | 10

DUX LAGER

Light golden beer with a citrus hop bouquet over a malty, biscuit-like aroma. Malty middle palate, slightly sweet, with enough hop to give a dry twinge at the end. Light and pleasant.

4 10

HEREFORD BITTER

Copper/amber with a nuts and mealy malt bouquet and a slight whiff of hops. Good hit of flavour and a nice spread of tasty, sweet malt and hops through to the finish, which is clean and slightly sweet with malt. Clear, tidy, flavourful beer.

5 10

NOR'WESTER PALE ALE

Amber/brassy colour, open, light head and softly malty nose with a whisk of ripe hops make a very appealing introduction to this beer. There is a slight pong, too, that gives it character, but not too much. Flavours are a polite mix of dry hops and sweet, light malt, with meal and nuts, finished by a gentle bitterness that tidies the end nicely.

6 10

SOU'WESTER STOUT

Dark, rich coffee-cream head and coffee in the bouquet too, along with nuts and toast and a subtle chocolate touch. Tastes as if it has been in a wooden barrel, which is highly unlikely, giving a flatness to the flavour and a yeasty, woody finish.

3 10

EAST WEST
BREWERY

Address 6 Tenahaun Place, Sockburn, Christchurch

Phone 03 341 3229, 0800 327 893

Website www.eastwestbrewery.co.nz

Available for tastings Yes

Opening hours 8am – 5pm, Monday – Friday

Tours Yes, by arrangement

Regional brewery providing big brand alternatives in the Canterbury region. Beers only available on draught from selected pubs, cafes and clubs around Christchurch.

MATSONS GOLD LABEL LAGER

Gold with a fresh white head. Crisp, malty bouquet with a slight mineral tang and a hint of hops. Simple malt palate, clean and fresh with a soft finish that is touched by hop flavours without bitterness.

 4 | 10

FORGE DRAUGHT

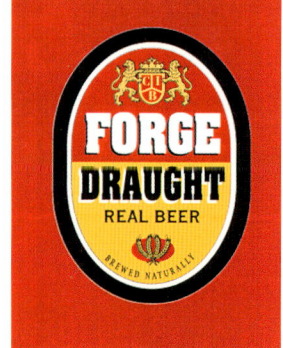

Light amber with a good, soft head. Malty bouquet is rather reserved but crisp and nicely trimmed with an aromatic, slightly herbal hop note. Nice light but pleasantly complex malt palate, soft and lightly hopped with a fine balance that leaves a dry finish, just astringent enough to be inviting. Crisp, clean, polite.

 5 | 10

MATSONS CLASSIC DRAUGHT

Pretty red amber with a lightly creamy white head. Hop aromas on the bouquet are light but defining, with clear, warm, delicately aromatic malt in support, hinting at shortbread. Soft, warm malt palate is light, well balanced and fresh, with a very light, clean finish. Light sweetness ends nicely dry.

 4 | 10

MATSONS PREMIUM DARK

Deep, very dark, red hued amber with a light beige head. Toasty, banana touched, roasted nut bouquet is aromatic and warm, with a fresh, sweet malt note that suggests warm chocolate cake. Crisp, fresh impact is very appealing, with nice nutty/toasty flavours in support, a slight ruff of astringency in the mid palate that turns dry at the end and more soft, delicate chocolate hints. Another, light fresh styled beer with balance and a finish that invites another glass.

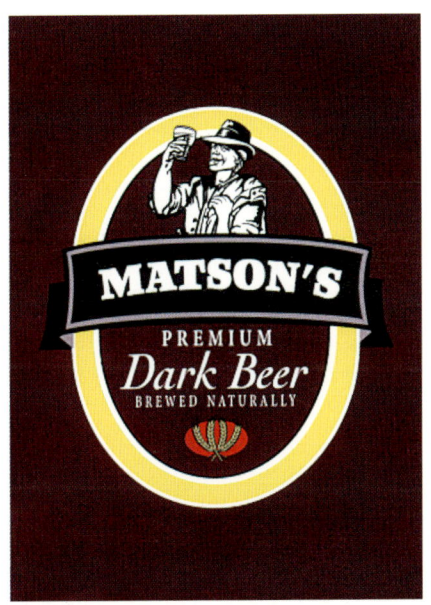

ROBSON
BREWING CO.

Timaru micro established in 2001 has rapidly built up a strong local following for its beers.

Address 21 Butler St, Timaru

Phone 03 688 1060

Available for tastings Yes

Opening hours 4pm – 6pm, Monday – Thursday; 3pm – 7pm Friday; 11am – 7pm Saturday; also open by special prior arrangement

Tours Yes, by arrangement

ROBSON GOLD

Lively gold with an open, fresh white head. Banana filled nose with some sweet malt notes and a pleasant dash of hops, followed by a sweet, malty palate with more banana and a dry tang of hops at the finish. Pleasant.

 3 10

ROBSON DRAUGHT

Jolly amber coloured beer with a crisp white head and a biscuity malt aroma tickled with a touch of herbal/floral hops. Charming malty palate is fresh and clean with a hint of hop flavour and a dryish, mellow finish. Softly pleasant.

 4 10

THE CUTTER PALE ALE

Copper coloured with a creamy white head and dashing bouquet high on hops, based on sweet, grainy malt. Malt hit on the palate is followed by a dry, flavoursome middle with biscuit and grain malt characters, some banana, and a touch of leafy hops with a dry twist of hop at the finish that tidies up its malty aftertaste. Dry, tasty beer with character and style.

 6 10

BLACK TOM

Deep, dark red tinted amber with a steep creamy head.
Bouquet is invitingly malty, lightly toasted and flecked with
citrus nuances, followed by a deep, toasty palate that has a
fresh quality and lightly creamy texture. There is a tang of
citrus at the finish, some cocoa characters and a generally
charming attitude to what is a soft, fine-flavoured beer.

HARRINGTON'S
BREWERY, CHRISTCHURCH

Address 199 Ferry Road, Christchurch

Phone 03 366 6323

Website www.harringtonsbrewery.co.nz

Available for tastings Yes, by arrangement

Opening hours 10am – 8pm, Monday – Friday

Tours Yes, by arrangement

This mid-sized Christchurch brewery, with a branch in Nelson producing similar and local brews, and reasonable distribution has given the northern South Island a greater opportunity to experience craft brewing than any other region in New Zealand. Established in 1991, but with links to a much older brewing tradition in the South Island, Harrington's has a wide but reliable range of beers, a highly professional brewer, and a good track record at competitions in New Zealand and Australia.

HARRINGTON'S BEST BITTER

Amber beer with an attractive head and lovely, delicate aroma that is malt based, slightly nutty and fine. There are nuts and clean malt on the palate, too, with an intriguing tinge of coffee, good weight and volume of flavour and a lengthy, malty finish. Quite soft beer, with a very minor hop role, but enough to give it shape and crisp up the finish. A smart drink, this.

 7 10

HARRINGTON'S BIG JOHN

Light amber, with an open head and ripe, fruity, mildly aromatic nose. Nutty, malty palate with good texture and lovely weight that delivers warmth and a sense of generosity. Nice dry, lightly hoppy finish provides length and more of that distinctive nuttiness. A convivial beer with real charm.

 6 10

HARRINGTON'S FINEST LAGER

Golden brew with a light, open head and a fresh, citric bouquet touched by fruit and a slightly herbal hop note. Refreshing clean first mouthful develops into a pure, malt and hop flavoured palate that is long and dry, with a lingering herbal/citric bitterness. Bright, lively well-constructed beer.

HARRINGTON'S KIWI DRAUGHT

Nice amber colour, light headed, mildly malty beer. Clean and simple, slightly sweet.

HARRINGTON'S NGAHERE GOLD

Golden colour, good, open head and a unusually sweet, light bouquet. The palate is malty, yet crisp and dry edged with a mildly citric/herbal character and good weight. Nice length, too, with a slightly austere character leaving a dry impression.

HARRINGTON'S STOUT

Dark, black-tinged with a good, coffee cream coloured head and a toasty nose that has a hint of iron about it. Flavours are positive; toasty/nutty malt with char and an astringent tang that elevates the aroma and draws out the finish so that the burned character lingers dry and flavourfully. Nicely made beer, satisfying, but more like porter than stout.

HARRINGTON'S TASMAN LAGER

Golden beer with a big head and a mildly aromatic citrus hop bouquet mellowed by malt. Has cut and lift, with a malty, sweetish, mild mid palate flavour concluded with a long, hoppy finish that has a dash of complexity. With some extra middle palate flavour and interest this could be very smart indeed.

 5 10

HARRINGTON'S WHEAT BEER

Light coloured with a creamy head and a sweetish, mildly spicy nose. Clean, citrus, lightly spiced mild taste finishes crisp and fresh. Pretty stuff.

 4 10

HARRINGTON'S WHOLE MALT DARK

Dark coloured with a light head and slightly creamy, toasty bouquet. Light palate has good toast and a hint of nutty malt. Surprisingly light, pleasant, dry finishing beer.

 3 10

HARRINGTON'S WHOLE MALT DRAUGHT

Amber with a light head and a strange, yeasty character on the nose. The palate is malty, slightly sweet and mellow. Best part is the finish, malt-flavoured and well-balanced.

 3 10

HARRINGTON'S WHOLE MALT LAGER

Golden with an open head and light, sweet, vaguely fruity nose. Very light, dry mid palate with a vague hop touch at the end.

 2 10

MILKSHED
BREWING CO.

Small brewery making mainstream beer lookalikes.
Draught sold as takeouts.

BLACK UDDER ALE

Dark with a creamy head and toasty, malty, roasted nut
bouquet with some vague hop notes. Toasty palate, with a
florid yeast character, good flavour depth and weight, and
a nice light touch at the finish leaving a clean, bright,
malty aftertaste. Very attractive, unique beer.

DEAD DAISY EXTRA STRENGTH PALE ALE

Amber coloured ale with a moderate head, a nice malt
character on the nose, and a whisk of hops, all confused
somewhat by a peculiar, slightly murky yeast note. Good
palate texture and some charming flavours of malt and
lightly herbal hops that leave a fresh, clean impression.
Dryish, mid weight beer.

MILKSHED ALE

Darkish, with a light, toasty nose and some florid yeast
characters that have a slightly sour edge. Sweetish, nutty,
simple, with a clean finish. Mild, no nonsense beer.

Address Cnr Davidsons and
Greenpark Roads, RD 4,
Greenpark, Christchurch

Phone 03 325 5711

Available for tastings No

Opening hours 12pm – 6pm

MILKSHED DRAUGHT

Amber, loose headed, very malty, classic NZ draught style complete with a dash of unusual, florid yeast sourness. Sweet, malty, soft mid palate and a submerged raft of mellow hops. Soft, sweetish, mild finish.

MILKSHED GOLD LAGER

Deep gold with a loose head and malty, clean nose. Sweet, nutty/malty mid palate, fresh tasting with good weight/ flavour balance. Charming stuff.

MILKSHED LAGER

Deep gold, brassy, with more of that florid yeast character. Light, malty, semi-dry, short and hard.

MONTEITH'S
BREWING CO.

Established in 1858 by the Monteith family, whose Phoenix Brewery was a stronghold of West Coast brewing culture by the end of the century. Under prohibition pressure, Phoenix merged into the conglomerate Westland Brewing Company.

The company is now a division of DB who facilitated a nationwide renaissance of interest in its characterful beers that reflect well on New Zealand's brewing history. A portion of the brand's production is made at DB's Otahuhu brewery.

Address Cnr Turamaha & Herbert Streets, Greymouth

Phone 03 768 4149

Website www.monteiths.co.nz

Available for tastings No

Opening hours 8am – 4.30pm, Monday – Friday

Tours 10am, 11.30am and 2pm, Monday – Friday

MONTEITH'S BLACK

Moderately dark coloured with a coffee-cream, loose head and more coffee on the nose, which is char lined, toasty, with a hint of liquorice. Very tasty mid palate, nicely constructed and balanced between a lemony bitterness and roasted nut, coffee, orange peel flavours. Soft finishing, milder than expected, it is a real charmer for all its macho appearance.

 7 | 10

MONTEITH'S CELTIC RED

Creamy pale head and a bright copper/amber colour lead to a ripe, hop-flecked bouquet, nutty, malty and aromatic. There is a dollop of toast on impact, and excellent malt flavours as the palate develops, with suave texture and a frill of flowery hops. Well spread, with a sweet dash at the finish, this is smart, tasty beer.

 7 | 10

MONTEITH'S GOLDEN LAGER

Gold coloured, light headed, fresh, nutty, malty smelling, malt tasting beer with a rich side salad of yeast and a nutty aftertaste. Mild, attractive, easy going beer.

 4 10

MONTEITH'S ORIGINAL ALE

Deep amber with an open, soft head and ripe, slightly floral, malt infused bouquet. Complex flavours amongst the malt and ripe hop notes, and there is a touch of nuts as well. Interesting, harmonious beer with good texture and balance, and a mild, neatly dry finish that lingers pleasantly.

 6 10

MONTEITH'S PILSNER

Golden beer, that smells fine and fragrant, with a slash of citrus hops amidst its malt tones. Fresh, soft, slightly austere, herb fringed palate with a clean, bright finish, this is well-balanced, pretty beer.

 5 10

MONTEITH'S SAISON

Attractive, amber coloured beer with a lightly creamy head and an intense, aromatic, spicy, nutty, citrus fresh bouquet. The flavour is big and quite complex, with nuts, malt, biscuits, meal beneath a wave of citrus-like, bristly hops that leave a lingering, dry, tasty wake. Very good beer, with lovely texture to match its flavour performance, and a good balance between sweet components and austerity. Delicious, thoughtful.

 8 10

MONTEITH'S SUMMER ALE

Golden with a light head and a spicy, fragrant nose that is perfumed with pomander-like characters. Clean, pure, quite deep flavours, spicy and ripely citrus in character, underpinned by clean malt. Finish is long, dry, spicy, with a gaggle of flavour details and a good sense of balance.

MINER'S
BREWERY

Alan and Jo Absolom revived one of New Zealand's richest brewing traditions when they and their partners opened Miner's Brewery on the West Coast in 1993. Their beers have become part of the local community in the interim, with whole malt beers that aim for popular appeal yet depend on craft basics such as complex malts and prime hops.

Address 10 Lyndhurst St, Westport

Phone 03 789 6201

Available for tastings Yes

Opening hours 10.30am – 5.30pm, Monday – Saturday

Tours 11.30am and 1.30pm

BARRACOUDA PILSNER

Gold with a good close head. Fragrant head has a citrus tang to it and inviting, plump malt that is clear and clean. Fresh palate with lovely, crisp malt flavours and a light hop presence that leaves a tinge of dryness at the finish. Crisp, lively, lightweight lager.

  6 10

MINER'S DRAUGHT

Copper gold with a creamy, light head. Aromatic, hop riddled malty nose with an interesting almost fruity, tang to it. Light, malty palate is crisp and pure with a soft texture and faint twist of hops that jumps in right at the end. Attractive, honest, refreshing beer.

 6 10

MINER'S DARK

Deep, dark amber with a touch of brown and a rich, coffee cream head. Toasty nose has moments of coffee and a real tang of molasses and marmite, with depth and a light richness. Lovely texture is light with a very mellow character and fresh nature that complements the toasty, ripe malt flavours. Clean, crisp finishing with a dry tail and hints of roasted nuts. Well-balanced, light, fresh beer.

GREEN FERN
BREWERY

One beer brewery label wholly owned and produced by Miner's, this is one of the few certified organic (Bio-Gro) beers in the country.

GREEN FERN PREMIUM LAGER

Brassy gold with a pleasant, loose head. Big, leafy, herbal hop aromas on the nose with a hearty dollop of fresh malt make for a bold impression and the palate delivers a flavourful lager with some nice mid palate hop texture, crisp malt flavours and enough bitterness in the malty finish to leave a lingering aftertaste of sweet biscuit malt and slightly herby hops. Tasty, crisp, lively lager.

Address 10 Lyndhurst St, Westport

Phone 03 789 6253

Available for tastings Yes

Opening hours 10.30am – 5.30pm, Monday – Saturday

Tours 11.30am and 1.30pm

GOOD BASTARDS
BREWERY

Address 10 Lyndhurst St, Westport

Phone 03 789 6201

Available for tastings Yes

Opening hours 10.30am – 5.30pm, Monday – Saturday

Tours 11.30am and 1.30pm

The label claims it is the world's most humorous beer, with "More laughs per session on this than any other beer on the planet."

GOOD BASTARDS LAGER

Light gold with a loose white head. Fresh, lightly citrus/herbal nose with some charming malt characters. Fresh palate is zippy with citrus and crisp malt, light and clean finishing. Attractive thirst quencher, if you drink it by yourself you get a smile, but no laughs.

6 10

GOOD BASTARDS DARK

Deep, dark amber brown with a light coffee head. Roasted, toasty, aromatic bouquet with a hint of malt extract, quite crisp in spite of its warmth. Light, fresh toasty, roasted palate with light malt flavours and a gentle quality. Very drinkable, tasty finishing, mild beer with a final fresh flick.

6 10

WANAKA
BEERWORKS

Classy small operation based in the warplane museum at Wanaka airport, its bottled beers deserve a much wider support than they get in Central Otago and further afield. Brewski in particular has the potential to become the beer of Central's Pinot Noir set, much as Coopers has captured the palates of South Australia's winemakers.

A new (established 1998) operation with huge potential.

Address Wanaka Transport Museum, SH6, RD2, Wanaka

Phone 03 443 1865

Website www.nzsouth.co.nz/ wanakabeerworks/

Available for tastings Yes

Opening hours 9am – 6pm, Monday – Friday

Tours 2pm

BREWSKI

Light golden beer, fragrant with a citric hop character and solid, malty background. Full flavoured, malty, nutty palate with a clean, brisk hop character, excellent length and texture, and good substance. The dry, lingering finish has just enough hops to leave a bright impression. Very clean and fresh beer.

 7 10

CARDRONA GOLD

Bright copper colour with a light head. Malty, slightly herbal, sweetish aroma and a flat, slightly florid yeast note. Light, malty palate, well flavoured but short on texture. Sweetish, mild finish.

 4 10

SPITFIRE PALE ALE

Brightly golden beer with a light, malty nose, a tinge of floral hops and a discrete freshness. Open, crisp palate with good flavours of ripe malt/nuts and a strong hop presence that gives it real momentum through to the lingering, dry, nuts and hop finish. Well-structured beer with mellow flavours balancing the hops.

6 **10**

TALL BLACK

Very dark amber with an open, cream coloured head and toasty, mineral bouquet that hints at chocolate. Good flavour weight with nice roasted malt/nutty notes and a light toast. Quite light bodied, with a dryish finish that holds some of the nuts and toast for later.

5 **10**

OTAGO
BREWPUB

Microbrewery currently operating out of the Ski Hut restaurant and bar in Queenstown.

WAKATIPU DARK

Dark coloured, with a light head and subdued, honey tinged nose that is malty and quite complex. Malty palate has a touch of class about it, with coffee touched, toasty flavours that are lighter than the colour suggests, with a dry, hop touched finish. Clean, fresh appealing beer.

5 **10**

WAKATIPU GOLD

Soft, malty beer with a strong theme of florid yeast and sweetness. Light.

1 **10**

WAKATIPU MOONLIGHT

Bland, light, malt touched, with the taste of old yeast.

1 **10**

WAKATIPU WHEAT

Pale, with a very light head and sweet, lightly aromatic nose. Flavour is fat with wheat character, grainy, soft and mild, with a clean finish. Attractive drinking.

4 **10**

Address 14 Church St, Queenstown

Phone 03 442 9688

Available for tastings Yes

Opening hours 11.30am 'til 2.30am, 7 days

Tours Yes, by arrangement

EMERSON'S
BREWING CO.

Address 9 Grange St, Dunedin

Phone 03 477 1812

Website
www.emersonsbrewery.co.nz

Available for tastings No

Opening hours 10am –
5.30pm, Monday – Friday;
11am – 2pm, Saturday
(Summer only)

Tours Yes, by arrangement

In recent years this brewery has emerged as one of the stars of New Zealand's brewing renaissance. Since Richard Emerson began brewing at his tiny Dunedin brewery in 1992, he has produced a steady stream of well constructed, characterful beers, many of which are already New Zealand classics.

EMERSON'S 1812 INDIA PALE ALE

Pure copper coloured with a fine, buff head. Its big, aromatic bouquet is spiked with hops and a citrus lilt, with mellow, complex malt underneath. A hint of nuts too, it is an invitation to drink. The flavour delivers, fine and medium bodied with quite rich malt, a little citrus note and long, pure, clean flavours, twitched with a brisk hop austerity that delivers a lingering, dry, flavourful finish. Top class beer, almost a style apart, in spite of its name, with finesse and freshness. Is this the beginning of a true New Zealand beer style?

 9 10

EMERSON'S BOOKBINDER BITTER

Dark copper-colour and a creamy head introduces this mellow, charming beer. It has a fruity, citrus scented hop bouquet with a moderating malt sweetness and a fresh, warm yeast character. Mid weight beer, its flavour delightfully balanced between mellow maltiness/mild spice, yeast and crisp hop astringency without intruding on the general softness of the beer. Good, clean, flavoursome finish.

 8 10

EMERSON'S ORGANIC PILSNER

Light copper gold. Light, fine head. Wonderful citrus and hop bouquet is open, pure, and tantalising. Has a background of mellow, light malt and a hint of stink that is intriguing, creamy. Lovely, clean flavour impact, leading to a remarkably delicate palate, with a suave middle and very long, lingering finish, tinged with bitterness and a nice hint of orange peel. Beautiful beer, poised, detailed and yet with a sense of clarity

 9 **10**

EMERSON'S OATMEAL STOUT

Black with a deep mahogany flicker. Loose, creamy head. Toasty, ripe bouquet that is remarkably fresh and dancing with chocolate tweaked by a nutty hint and tinge of citrus. Good, rich impact of creamy, nutty, toasty flavours with an unusually light middle, but the flavours have legs and stretch through to a fresh, nutty finish that has a real orange tang to it. Nice beer, with a strain of chocolate character that is very appealing.

 8 **10**

EMERSON'S OLD '95

Deep amber, creamy head. Ripe, orange and spice and malt bouquet followed by a fizzy burst of flavour that is spicy, and orangey/fruity with weight, substance and spread followed by a long, serious drive off the end. It promises to be sweet with such a concoction of flavour, then delivers dryness and a lingering spicy freshness. Terrific stuff, but one is enough, for this is a strong, special beer that would be wonderful with a hearty meal.

 8 **10**

EMERSON'S MARIS GOLD

Golden amber. Good, fine, dense head and a mellow, malty, soft nose with a faint hop twist. Malty beer with a slight mid palate sweetness and soft, mealy/nutty finish. Malt-based, charming, easy going style with a clean finish tweaked by a shadow of hop.

 5 | 10

EMERSON'S WEISSBIER HEFE-WEIZENBIER

Slightly cloudy, open light head, brushed golden colour. Creamy, citrus tinged, light, charming nose with some acetone/banana hints followed by good flavour; positive, creamy, delicately complex with a sweet note and foamy bubble. Clean. Could do without the foam, but nice beer all the same. Dry finish gives it a lift.

 6 | 10

EMERSON'S TAIERI GEORGE

Dark beer with the smell of a pomander, fine and dusty like an old book, with a luxury of spice and orange peel. It feels big and rich yet is surprisingly delicate in its detail and subtle nuances of flavour, and manages to finish fresh and almost dry. Nice beer.

 7 | 10

EMERSON'S LONDON PORTER

Solid, black with a creamy, open head. Fragrant, toasty, crisp malt and citrus hop bouquet. Inviting. Toasty, dark, flavourful, yet middle weight beer for all its dark promise, but the hops give it drive and there is enough flavour to maintain depth. A trace of sweetness at the finish.

 6 | 10

McDUFFS
BREWERY

Casual, mid-town Dunedin brewer selling take-away draught. Established 1992.

MCDUFFS DARK ALE

Dark with a very light head and an aromatic, toasty/coffee nose that manages to be fresh as well as warm. Coffee/toast palate with dry malt characters is mellow and pleasant. Light, well balanced, easy paced beer.

 4 10

MCDUFFS BLACK DIAMOND

Darkish, with a light, open head and malty, warm, vaguely orange peel nose. Mild, with a malty mid palate and clean, warm finish.

 3 10

MCDUFFS EDINBURGH DRAUGHT

Amber beer with aromatic sweet malt and florid, slightly sour yeast nose. Cereal-like flavours are clean and simple, with a malt mellowness at the finish.

 3 10

MCDUFFS CLASSIC GOLD (WHEAT)

Clean, sweetly aromatic bouquet with a pungent wheat note. Sweet middle palate, very light with a dryish finish. Chunky, simple.

 2 10

Address 695 Great King Street, Dunedin

Phone 03 477 7276

Available for tastings Yes

Opening hours 10.30am – 8pm, Monday – Saturday

Tours Yes, by arrangement

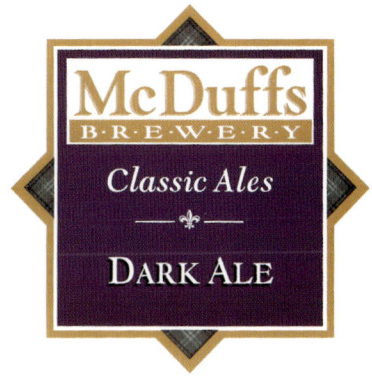

MCDUFFS BLACK VELVET LIMITED EDITION

Darkish, with a whisky barrel nose tweaked by banana, toast and coffee nuances. Light, woody mid palate with a dash of complexity. Very dry, light finish.

2 | 10

MCDUFFS ORIGINAL ALE

Amber, with a big, open head and sweet, malty nose touched by a florid yeast character. Simple, beery flavours are fresh and pleasant.

2 | 10

SPEIGHT'S
BREWERY

One of New Zealand's great breweries, established in Dunedin in 1876, it rapidly became the largest brewery in Otago, and the largest in the country in 1923, when it joined the New Zealand Breweries amalgamation with Lion, Hancock and Co, Staples, and others.

Now a brand of Lion, it is no longer exclusively brewed in Dunedin, instead becoming an extension of the advertising image as a rural southern bloke's brew. The recent return to special batch brewing and revival of traditional, kauri equipment suggests that the company's future may be more substantial, with the sort of characterful beers that once made it the nation's number one.

Address 200 Rattray Street, Dunedin

Phone 03 477 9480

Available for tastings No

Opening hours 8.30am – 5pm, Monday – Friday

Tours 10am, 11.45am, 2pm and 7pm, Monday – Thursday; 10am, 11.45am and 2pm, Friday – Sunday

SPEIGHT'S DISTINCTION ALE

Deep amber. Close head. Light coffee, roasted nut/coffee and ripe malt aromas are warm and convivial, with a high hop note, ripe, mellow, with a passing honey character. Good mid palate, very malty, richly complex and well shaped with a good hop twinge keeping the end honest. Good beer, well balanced, warm, complex. Very sweet.

SPEIGHT'S PALE ALE

Deep gold. Light, close head. Aromatic, gently spicy, herbs and citrus/floral hop note. Malt hints. Very soft front palate, mellow, charming, nicely balanced. Soft, malty, charming finish is slightly sweet with a dry edge and some citrus tones.

SPEIGHT'S DRAUGHT

Light copper amber with a close, light head. Simple, malty nose, just touched with hops. Soft, biscuits and vanilla palate, light finish, easy, mild.

3 | 10

SPEIGHT'S OLD DARK 5 MALT ALE

Deep copper/amber beer. Deep chocolate malt bouquet, ripe, soft, voluptuous, hints of toast and coffee, with a mineral buzz. Warm sweet front stuffed with complex malt character, well balanced and charming, with good momentum and a long, light, delicate twist of hops at the very end. Delicious, perfectly balanced, lingering sweet.

7 | 10

SPEIGHT'S PORTER

Dark, copper-tinged beer with a pale cream head and a toasty, ripely malty aroma with just a faint hint of hops. Tastes immediately malty, with a pleasantly creamy softness that toughens up to finish quite crisp with a toffee-like flavour tinged with a gentle astringency. Very attractive, surprisingly light beer.

7 | 10

SPEIGHT'S PILSNER

Light gold with a close, pleasing head and a lightly fragrant nose that has touches of flowers and citrus as well as a mild malt sweetness. Very pretty, crisp, charming beer with a delicate, creamy touch and lingering trace of malt infused bitterness.

7 | 10

INVERCARGILL
BREWERY

In a bright blue converted cowshed outside Invercargill, father and son team, Steve and Gerry Nally have built an impressive wee brewery that epitomises the enterprise and creativity of New Zealand's new brewing generation. Keep your eyes on this one.

Address 155 Oteramika Rd, Invercargill

Phone 025 932 056

Available for tastings Yes

Opening hours 11am – 3pm, Saturday or by arrangement

Tours Yes, by arrangement

BIMAN GOLDEN LAGER

Creamy close head and deep golden colour. Fresh, citrus-filled hop bouquet with a sweet malt note, crisp, full and enticing. Malty, very citrus-edged palate with fruity, almost tropical notes that linger through to the end, which has a clean, dryish touch to finish it and a full flow of malty charm. Different, but delicious.

 7 10

IBS EXTRA SPECIAL BITTER

Copper/red amber with a close, healthy looking head. Malty nose with floral, autumn ripe hop aromas and a mild, funky note that has hints of herbal hop in it. Lightly nutty, malty palate has a nice hop presence and a swathe of sweet malt that suggests freshly baked biscuits. Light, slightly creamy finish is rather light on hop bitterness for the name. A good beer, though.

 7 10

PITCH BLACK

Close, café crema head with dense, deeply black body showing a flash of dark amber. Dense, chocolaty bouquet with toasty (Vogel's) highlights and a nutty touch, licked with a dash of distant hops. Rich, deep palate has chocolate and toast flavours with a remarkable smoothness of character and supple touch. Tasty chocolate touches at the end, too, with a lingering dryness and interesting dab of orange. You can imagine the Bluff oysters sitting in Foveaux Strait just beyond the horizon, waiting to be invited to a feast.

WASP WEIZENBIER

Light white head, close with a light, golden colour. Quite a meaty, malty nose with a hint of honey and some fruity notes. A bit funky. Malty palate is light, mild, pleasant but short.

CHAPTER SIX

GUIDE TO IMPORTED BEER

So, given that nationalist sentiments are likely to be subverted by the large and rapidly expanding range of beer being offered around the country, here are some general tips about the styles you will find behind certain labels of imported beer. As for the actual beer evaluations in this book, it is fair to say this book is concentrating on what is made here, in part because what I may taste today could be gone tomorrow, never to be seen in the South Pacific again.

THE BASICS

At a practical level, beer comes in two sorts – draught and bottled.

DRAUGHT is what you buy in the pub, in a glass or in a bottle (pub pet, rigger, flagon) to take away. It is less likely to be pasteurised, and is frequently, but not always, less fizzy than the bottled version.

BOTTLED beer can find itself thousands of kilometres and many months away from its origins. Brewers often add preservatives, extra gas or pasteurise it to protect it from the temperature fluctuations, bottle shock and sun strike that can send it into flabby ignominy. But a million kilometres from Pilsen, it could be the only chance you have of tasting the Real Thing.

THE FAMOUS BEER STYLES

These are not meant to be used as a guide to New Zealand beers with similar names, or even as an evaluation of the various brands being offered. It is simply a rough indicator to what you can expect behind the label of a foreign brew.

ALE
Classically made from top fermenting yeasts, they are typically aromatic, malty, flavourful, copper coloured beers with a strong sense of their own character. Because of the yeast, they will also show a wide variety of idiosyncratic qualities that serve as interesting, often defining features.

ALTBIER
Old beer in German, meaning not one of the new-fangled lagers. Dark, hoppy, dry finishing beers with a good weight of malt.

Try   Diebels *Germany*
      Grolsch *Netherlands*
      Kirin *Japan*

BARLEY WINE
Sweetish, high alcohol, deeply coloured ale, often funky flavoured. Can be aged for a reasonable time in barrel, giving even more swagger to its character.

Try   Youngs *England*
      Samuel Adams *England*
      Fullers *England*
      Normans Conquest *England*
      Whitbread *England*

BELGIAN ALE
Usually malty, soft flavoured, copper coloured beers. Also includes brown (also called Flemish ale) and red ales that are piquant to a greater or lesser degree, and richly fruity, sometimes impressively so. Special is an ale too, but is somewhat different from its cousins.

BELGIAN SPECIAL
Sometimes called golden ale. Powerful, light seeming golden beer that has fruity characters and a hoppy departure that hides its substantial kick.

Try   Duvel

BIÈRE DE GARDE

Classy brews from northern France, next to the Belgian border. The name means the same for beer as it does for wine – beer worth keeping, when its powerful, spicy flavours mellow to complexity and fruity asides.

Try   Duyk
       Annoeullin
       Ch'ti
       St Omer

BITTER

Deep, copper coloured beer from the heart of Britain, its calling note is a hoppy bouquet and astringent tang. Because this is intended as a quaffing ale, it is usually lower in alcohol, although not so low as to compromise its flavour.

Try   Adnams *England*
       Eldridge Pope Thomas Hardy *England*
       Fullers *England*
       Marstons *England*
       Shepheard Neame *England*
       Tetley *England*
       Theakstons *England*
       Timothy Taylor *England*
       Youngs *England*

BLACK

A traditional seafarers' brew with origins in the Baltic, often flavoured with spruce. It may have been in Captain Cook's mind when he added spruce-like rimu to his original brew in Fiordland. Now a Japanese speciality, it is normally bitter and dry, with a good hop kick. Usually made clean using lager yeast.

Try   Asahi *Japan*
       Kirin *Japan*
       Sapporo *Japan*
       Suntory *Japan*

BOCK

This is beer made to celebrate barley, and it does so by being richly malty, almost creamy, with at least a trace of sweetness. Usually lager.

Try   Einbecker *Germany*
       Kulmbacher *Germany*
       Paulaner *Germany*
       Samichlaus *Germany*

BROWN ALE

Sweet, cuddly, malty beer, often nutty, frequently with a dash of hops to clean up the finish. Always nut brown, always richly flavoured. Northern England's are famous, and Belgian ones have a freshness than gives them real pizzazz.

Try   Samuel Smith *England*
       Newcastle *England*
       Brooklyn Brown *USA*
       Palm *Belgium*
       De Koninck *Belgium*
       Liefmans *Belgium*
       Rodenbach *Belgium*

DORTMUNDER

Famous in Europe where it has long been found in international hotels and restaurants. Deep golden coloured beer with a positive, nutty flavour and solid hop background, with a long, dry finish. Bottom fermented.

Try   Dab
       Dortmunder Union

DUNKEL

Copper coloured lagers from Munich, hoppy and often nutty, with spice features and a creamy textured substance moderated by ripe aromas and a dry, crisp finish. The best are fantastic and invariably served draught.

Try   König Ludwig *Germany*

FARO
Very rare, sweet lambic from Brussels.

Try   Lindemans *Belgium*

FRUIT BEER
Very popular in Belgium, where lambics already have a natural fruitiness. Normal beer is made from malt, and then the fruit is added, the beer gaining flavour and often astringency from the steeping process. Sometimes fruit beers are hopped, sometimes not. These beers are now growing in popularity around the world as consumers get a taste for the individuality possible from craft brewing.

Try   Boon Kriek *Belgium*
        Cantillon Framboise *Belgium*

GUEUZE
A Belgian classic, this is a lambic blend of fresh brews and an aged beer that is bottle fermented. Terrific, fresh and lightly creamy, with funky flavours controlled by a crisp edge. Can be wonderful. The wine comparisons go on and on, with one of the most popular producers being a firm called Lindemans.

Try   Lindemans *Belgium*

HELLES
The blonde version of Munich lager, usually soft and cuddly with mild hops, but dry at the end. Served draught in litre steins it is most impressive. Also used throughout Germany to describe any blonde brew, and it is a popular style with microbreweries around the world seeking to identify with Munich's traditions.

Try   Augustiner *Germany*

IMPERIAL STOUT
The famous beer of the Balkans, although it was originally made in Britain's northeast for export to its once close trading partners. Dark with

roasted, spicy, fruit tinted flavours invariably with a substantial charge of warming alcohol. The richest of beer, as the name implies, is now as likely to come from the Baltic fringe as it is from Britain.

Try   Courage *England*

INTERNATIONAL LAGER
The style founded by Carlsberg and imitated by any number of famous breweries that now boast the world's biggest beer brands – Heineken, Carlsberg, Stella Artois. Clean, crisp and pure flavoured with a collar of aromatic, mellow hops, they are reliably fine relief for a cosmopolitan thirst.

Try   Stella Artois
       Heineken

IPA
The original travelling beer of England, India Pale Ale was shipped to the Imperial Army in India to sustain the thin red line. Given extra alcohol and hops to last the journey out, this should be the hoppiest, driest, strongest version of bitter/pale ale that is England's great beverage.

Try   Worthington White Shield *England*

IRISH ALE
Sweetly malty, suave tasting beers, often nutty and lightly hopped, they are some of the most satisfyingly charming of all beers. A recent trend to charge them with nitrogen after the fashion of Guinness has muddied the style somewhat.

Try   Smithwicks

IRISH RED ALE
No different from above, but there is something poetic in the notion of Red Irish beer.

KÖLSCH
Reserved, pretty beer from Cologne in Germany, it usually has a mellow hop aroma, with delicate malt/fruit/hop flavours and a dry, lingering finish. Draught only and not exported, but a style worth remembering if you are ever in Cologne.

LAGER
Covers everything from Lion Red to Pilsner Urquell, and invariably applies to bottom fermented, cool brewed beers. Popular belief is that they are all golden, but some of the greats are dark. International lagers are the standards by which most are judged in contemporary culture, but the great ones are bristling with hops, fattened and enhanced by age into memorable drinks by any standard.

LAMBIC
The carefully husbanded, wild yeast beers found mainly in Belgium. Funky, fruity, emphatically individual.

Try   Boon *Belgium*

MARZEN
Ginger coloured lager from Vienna, this classic, aromatic style has a distinctive malty spice at its heart and rich hops all over it from start to finish. Fresh but simultaneously mellow, it is one of the most inviting inventions ever.

Try   Spaten *Germany*

MILD
The poor beer of British pubs, now almost vanished and forgotten, it was the malty, nutty, soft centred beer of the industrial Midlands working class before unscrupulous publicans destroyed its reputation by topping it with slops.

Try   Banks *England*, draught only

MILK STOUT

It was once common to add lactose to these dark, dense beers to sweeten them, hence the name, but generally these are the sweet stouts of England; ripe and creamy textured, sweet finishing beers of substance.

Try   Mackeson *England*
       Youngs *England*

OLD ALE

Rich, sweet, chocolate and malt filled beers with light hops and a fleshy quality; well crafted top fermented versions can be stunning. Too often they are sweet, malty and simple. Old is a style, not an indication of time spent gently maturing.

Try   Eldridge Pope Thomas Hardy *England*
       Theakstons *England*

PALE ALE

Although beer drinkers and brewers may argue long and hard over the distinction between pale ale and bitter, they are effectively so similar as to be the same style. The difference is in the label. This is fine textured, elegantly flavoured beer with a celebratory infusion of hops that gives it an aromatic fragrance, a firm, structural bitterness, and long, austere, flavour charged aftertaste. It is the epitome of top fermentation and hop craft.

Try   Marstons *England*
       Samuel Smith *England*
       Worthington White Shield *England*
       Bass *England*
       Morland Old Speckled Hen *England*
       Ind Coope *England*

PILSNER

What pale ale/bitter is to top fermentation, Pilsner is to lager, the elegant aristocrat with hoppy finesse and detailed, lingering flavour. Crisp and softly, delicately creamy centred, long and dry they can be exhilarating. Probably the most copied beer style on earth, at least in litres sold.

Try   Jever *Germany*
       Budejovice Budvar *Czech*
       Bitburger *Germany*
       Christoffel *Netherlands*
       Gambrinus *Czech*
       Pilsner Urquell *Czech*

PORTER

The great beer of old London, this hoppy chappie is as black as possible, deeply flavoured but with poise rather than richness. Invariably has toasty, nutty characters and a mellow fruitiness, with hop panache front and backm leaving dry, lightly charred traces behind.

SMOKED BEER

Rauchbier in Germany, the style uses smoked malt to impart a fume to their beers. Can be wonderfully exotic.

Try   Aecht Schlenkerla *Germany*

ROGGEN

Made from rye, rather than barley, it has a rustic, mealy quality. Also called sahti when it is flavoured with juniper in eastern Europe.

Try   Schierlinger *Germany*

SAISON

Belgian ale usually fresh and spicy in character with mellow maltiness and a fruit-like finish. Sometimes flavoured with spices. Often sold bottle aged from the previous autumn, they are invariably big and warm.

SCOTTISH ALE

Big, malty beer with minimum hops, these come in a range from light coloured to deep, dark brown. Top fermented, mellow and warm, often strong to boot.

Try   MacAndrews
       McEwan
       Caledonian
       Traquair

SPARKLING ALE

Popular in Adelaide, this is Australia's contribution to the world's brewing traditions. Mellow malted with a hard edge of hops and bustle of complex, lively flavour details that is very refreshing, this pale, golden beer is bottle conditioned in the traditional Australian manner, making it one of the rare examples of bottle beer being better than the draught original.

Try   Coopers *Australia*

STEAM BEER

California Steam is fermented in shallow vats to keep cool and get the greatest benefit from the lager yeasts they use. The result is malty, crisply hoppy, very charming beer with a gentle manner and a dry finish.

Try   Anchor

STOUT

Most famous as Guinness, these black, creamy, richly flavoured, char, chocolate and roasted nut beers can be aromatically dry and bitter in the Guinness tradition, or sweet (milk stout).

Try   Beamish *Ireland*
       Guinness *Ireland*
       Murphy *Ireland*
       Whitbread *England*
       Youngs *England*

TRAPPIST

Another great bottle conditioned style, this one is made in six Trappist monasteries in Belgium and the Netherlands. Usually sweet, always fragrant and ripe, fruity beers, richly complex and strong. Top fermented, but with as much character as lambic, if not the wickedness.

Try   Chimay
       Orval
       Rochefort
       Schaapskooi

Westmalle
Westvleteren

VIENNA LAGER
Also called Marzen, sometimes Oktoberfestbier; jazzy copper coloured,
malt soft, hop licked lager of great style.

WHEAT OR WEISSBIER
Beer made from wheat in any number of styles, but usually light and
refreshing, often sweet and fruity. Popular in Belgium, where it is often
tarted up with orange peel, in Germany and, with considerable success, in
New Zealand.

Try   Hoegaarden *Belgium*
       Erdinger Weissbier *Germany*
       Redback *Australia*

WITBIER
Witbier or bière blanche is Belgian white beer made from wheat, usually
cloudy and infused with orange peel and coriander. Not all of the wheat is
malted for the process, and the finished beers are firm and fresh. Most
famous is Hoegaarden.